MW00695721

THE DESIRE TO SERVE

Book design by Adam Robinson

Published by The Greenleaf Center for Servant Leadership
133 Peachtree St. NE, Suite 350
Atlanta, GA 30303

www.greenleaf.org

THE DESIRE TO SERVE

SERVANT LEADERSHIP FOR FIRE AND EMERGENCY SERVICES

by

Dr. Eric James Russell
Foreword by Dr. Don M. Frick

The Greenleaf Center for Servant Leadership
Atlanta, Georgia

For my Wife

CONTENTS

Foreword   1

Acknowledgements   7

Chapter 1   9
Introduction

Chapter 2   17
The Roots of Servant Leadership

Chapter 3   25
The Characteristics of Servant leadership

Chapter 4   41
The Constructs of Servant Leadership and
the Fire and Emergency Services

Chapter 5   47
Agapao Love

Chapter 6   55
Humility

Chapter 7   63
Altruism

Chapter 8   69
Vision

Chapter 9   79
Trust

Chapter 10   89
Empowerment

Chapter 11   99
Service

References

About the Author

FOREWORD

PEOPLE WHO ASK FOR AN EXAMPLE OF A SERVANT-LEADER NEED look no further than their local firefighters, emergency medical technicians, and other first responders. They are part of the same tribe as Danny Suhr.

Mr. Suhr was the first firefighter killed on 9/11 when he was hit by a falling human body while running *toward* the danger. "He didn't look scared," said fellow firefighter Tony Sanseviro, "but he knew it was bad." Seven firefighters from Engine Company 216 rushed to his aid, which meant they were not in the South Tower when it collapsed. Even in death, Danny Suhr saved lives.

No one who watched the horrific events of 9/11 unfold can forget the images of other firefighters who bravely charged into the burning towers to help others escape. They, too, knew it was bad, but did not look scared—more like grimly determined—knowing that even if they were doomed, they would have lived the lives of heroic service they had chosen. Forty-three emergency medical technicians (EMTs) and paramedics perished along with 343 firefighters that day. Could there be any better examples of servant-leaders, people who are respected as leaders because they choose to serve first?

9/11 is the most vivid example of the courage and devotion so evident in those who work in fire and emergency services, but you can see other examples of that same competence and altruism every day in every state. Firefighters are consistently listed in the top three of the most respected professions in America. Not many others can say that.

If you want to learn lessons from any discipline, first listen to the experts like Eric Russell, the author of this book. Dr. Russell has spent a lifetime in fire and emergency services. In the Air Force, he was on teams that extinguished—or prevented—fires, and responded to every type of emergency imaginable. Both active duty military and department of defense civilian, he was a trainer and a leader. Eric retired as a Department of the Air Force Fire and Emergency Services Captain and to this day shares his knowledge by consulting Aircraft Rescue Fire Fighting (ARFF) organizations. He has taught more university courses on fire services and disaster management than most people take for their undergraduate majors. He has a passion for serving people in emergency situations and the knowledge of how to do it. That passion led Eric to servant leadership because Robert Greenleaf's philosophy expresses the values that Eric had always felt, deep down, were important when acting as a servant and as part of a servant-based organization.

Although Dr. Russell wrote this book to share the power of servant leadership with colleagues who work in fire and emergency services, his compelling behind-the-scenes glimpses of emergency work and explanations of enduring leadership principles make it useful for workers, managers, and leaders in every profession. Eric helps you smell the smoke and experience the confusion of a fire scene, but then shows why the style of leadership that is effective in an emergency situation is not nearly as appropriate back at the firehouse or hospital. He uses mountains of research and decades of experience to hold a mirror to the perils of bureaucracy and the confusion of leadership verses management functions that seem to exist at every workplace. That's why the case studies will seem familiar whether you are a firefighter, marketer, account executive, or simply a loyal employee trying to survive institutional dysfunction.

Dr. Russell understands that servant leadership is not just another academic theory or model of leadership, a quick-fix set of bullet points to rejigger our thinking about how to lead. It is a grounding *philosophy* of leadership that helps, to paraphrase the poet Robert Frost, unite love and need in our personal and organizational lives. It is a philosophy that is both practical (outcomes can be measured) and visionary. It applies to all people of all faiths speaking all languages, because the desire to serve is universal.

Unless you are wise to the ways of academia, the difference between a philosophy and an academic theory of leadership may seem arcane and moot, but it is important to understand in order to appreciate what Eric has done in this book. The late Dr. Stephen Prosser wrote a brilliant essay to investigate the question of whether servant leadership was a philosophy or a theory (he concluded it was a philosophy), but let's summarize the main difference here.[1] *Philosophies* address "big picture" approaches to existence, ethics, religious, scientific, and human experience. *Theories* narrow the focus. They postulate the way things are in specific situations and then test variables in order to prove the hypothesis. The results of testable theories can be duplicated by others. Sometimes a philosophy will lead to one or more testable theories, and that has been the case in servant leadership studies. The best theories integrate the deeper insights of their corresponding philosophies. For example, in this book, Eric Russell cites the writings of Larry Spears and Kathleen Patterson as two thinkers who provided servant leadership-based theories

---

1   Prosser, Stephen. *Servant Leadership: More Philosophy, Less Theory*. Indianapolis: The Greenleaf Center for Servant Leadership, 2010.

that could be, and have been, tested and validated, and then applies the findings to the fire and emergency services.

The basics of the servant leadership philosophy are not especially hard to understand, but you wouldn't know that from some of the writing out there. Eric Russell makes it simple. After describing Robert Greenleaf's core idea, he uses Larry Spears' "Ten Characteristics of Servant-Leaders" to flesh out the implications of a servant mindset: listening as the premier skill of a servant-leader, the ethical use of power—with persuasion favored over coercion and manipulation, use of foresight based on informed intuition and reflection, building community, and other skills, capacities, and characteristics.

Then Dr. Russell uses Dr. Kathleen Patterson's "Seven Virtuous Constructs of Servant Leadership" to describe in detail how servant leadership applies to fire and emergency services. While the constructs—*agapao* love, humility, altruism, vision, trust, empowerment, and service—may seem abstract, the author will convince you that they are eminently practical and descriptive of the inner forces that animate professionals in this field to serve. That source of the desire to serve is the engine of spirit that Greenleaf called *entheos*, which comes from the same root as the word enthusiasm.

Reading this book, I wondered why more professions do not speak openly about the motive of servanthood or attempt to apply servant-inspired policies in their organizations. Maybe they are not as brave as firefighters like Eric Russell, because this is scary stuff to folks who consolidate, hoard, and wield power to satisfy ego-based needs. Servant leadership requires an inner journey that is scarier than not making a sales quota at the end of the year or going neck-in-neck for a promotion. In the words of Eric Russell: "Servant leadership is not ice cream for breakfast and the servant-leader is not a softy." It is not for the faint of heart.

At the end of his life, theologian Karl Barth was asked if he could summarize his life's work. By that time, Barth had published more than 600 works, which took up yards, and yards of space on a bookshelf, so he had a lot of summarizing to do. Here is what he said: "Jesus loves me, this I know, for the Bible tells me so." The words to an old gospel children's song cut through all the scholarship and got to the philosophy of his life's work.

Robert Greenleaf was never asked to summarize his life's work in a similar fashion, but I believe he did so anyway on two occasions. The first was on the fateful day in October 1968 when the phrase "servant-leader" first popped into his head and he told his wife Esther, "That phrase pretty much sums up everything I've been trying to communicate. I'm really talking about *love*, but that word has lost much of its meaning these days, so this may be a way to get people to listen." The second, similar summary came at the end of a series of five lectures he gave at Dartmouth in 1968: "Virtue and justice and order are good, but not good enough—not nearly good enough. In the end, nothing really counts but *love* and *friendship*."[2]

Eric Russell understands that *love* is at the heart of fire and emergency services: love of serving and saving lives and love of other precious humans. As for friendship, guess what? The practices of *first* listening to a friend non-judgmentally, caring for the other as much as for oneself, being present when a friend fails, and cheering when a friend learns and succeeds can be implemented into the workplace. Not overnight, not easily, but it has been done by nonprofits and businesses

2   Frick, Don M. *Robert K. Greenleaf: A Life of Servant Leadership.* San Francisco: Berrett Koehler, 2004, p. 271.

that follow the principles of servant leadership, while still demanding personal accountability. Eric Russell wants love and friendship to animate the people and policies of his profession, and so should you.

Don M. Frick
August 2013
Indianapolis, IN

ACKNOWLEDGEMENTS

THE PROCESS OF CREATING A BOOK TAKES TIME, PATIENCE, AND most of all guidance from others. I want to take this opportunity to thank the individuals who helped make this book come alive. First, I want to thank Dr. Don Frick for being my editor and guide in this process. It was an honor to have such an accomplished author and servant-leader walk with me through this journey; I am humbled and forever grateful. I want to thank CEO Joe Iarocci, Shirley Wyant, and LeAnne Yoder from the Robert K. Greenleaf Center for Servant Leadership for their willingness to turn this manuscript into a published book; I can never say thank you enough.

I want to thank Dr. Kathleen Patterson. Without her work on the seven constructs of servant leadership, this book would not have been possible. The very idea for this book leaped off the pages of her work. I want to thank Dr. Larry Spears, whose writing and research on servant leadership is a gift to all of us. Without his work, together with Robert Greenleaf's, servant leadership would not be where it is today.

In life, some of us have the opportunity to learn from exceptional individuals, individuals who give themselves in service to others. I want to acknowledge Fire Chief (ret.) Robert Schultz, a great example of a servant-leader within the fire and emergency services. I want to say thank you to Dr. Donna Kay Hansen of Grand Canyon University and Dr. Rodger Broomé of Utah Valley University for their friendship and willingness to mentor me. I also want to thank Father Martin

Diaz, O.P.; you are a true servant-leader who helps me find my path. In addition, I want to say thank you to the faculty, staff, and students at Utah Valley University's Department of Emergency Services, as well as the institution's leadership, for making it easy for me to love my profession.

I want to acknowledge all those who served, serve, and will serve within the fire and emergency services. Your service and sacrifice will never be in vain; your willingness to give your all to others will never be forgotten. Your work is the greatest example of humanity to others. This book is for you; I can only hope it lives up to the nobility of the profession itself.

I want to thank my mom and dad for being there for me, guiding me to this day. Your love and devotion to me is a gift; I love the both of you with all my heart. To my family and friends, you surround me with love and laughter, making my life rewarding.

To my wife, Jamie, my happiness and soul mate, you are my most treasured gift. The greatest opportunity I have ever received is the chance to love you forever with all my heart; my life would be meaningless without you by my side. Most of all, to my Lord and Savior Jesus Christ; I am unworthy of your mercy, yet you pour your blessings out on me. You are my salvation. All glory is yours.

CHAPTER 1

INTRODUCTION

"I have no ambition in this world but one, and that is to be a fireman. The position may, in the eyes of some, appear to be a lowly one; but we who know the work, which the fireman has to do, believe that his is a noble calling. Our proudest moment is to save lives."

– Chief Edward F. Croker, Fire Department of New York

IF YOU ARE READING THIS BOOK, THERE IS A BETTER THAN AVERAGE chance that you either serve or are aspiring to serve in some capacity within a fire and emergency services organization. This means you have at least asked yourself the question: *Who do I desire to be?* That leads to a second question: *Who am I now?* Are you already a servant to others or do you desire to be a servant to others? This, by the way, is the core of what it means to be a fire and emergency services professional—to be in service to others. Now a related question to ask yourself: *What type of a leader do I desire to be?* This question matters because the profession, unlike many in the private sector, promotes from within. An officer is rarely hired from outside the organization's ranks and almost never recruited from outside of the fire and emergency services profession. The fire and emergency services leader of tomorrow—maybe you or the person next to you—is the follower of today.[1] The problem is, the followers of today are not prepared for the leadership positions of tomorrow.[2]

Schools, organizations, and academies spend vast amounts of time and money honing the skills needed to function as a responder; in fact, a paramedic may not be ready for the field for several years. The fire and emergency services profession does a fantastic job developing recruits, and advanced responders and seems to agree on minimum standards all entry-level professionals must meet.[3] Yet, while professional development guidelines recommend certain levels of certification or degrees for specific levels, there are no standards or educational models for becoming leaders. This is also true for promotions, because the profession does not have a universal standard for promotion, or even a commonly shared approach to developing leaders.[4]

This is a lot to take in, especially if you are new to the career field. It is daunting to think the question *Who do I desire to be?* must be answered, followed then by a response to *What type of a leader do I desire to be?* And there's one more, because the second question demands yet another question that is critical: *What type of leader do I desire to follow?* Make no mistake: the moment you begin the journey to pursue a fire and emergency services career, you expose yourself to existing fire and emergency services leaders in academia, the training academy, and the field.

This exposure to leaders and leadership prompts you to begin forming your own leadership style because, a majority of the time, a person's leadership style is based upon nothing more than experiences with past leaders, the good and the bad.[5] With everything else going on in one's professional journey, it may seem trivial to take time and ponder such questions or read literature on leadership rather than focusing on more hands-on skills and technical information. Yet, the fire and emergency services profession is all about leadership *at every level*: from the single company, rescue unit, or ambulance that arrives on-scene to the chiefs of large metropolitan and federal departments.

Consider a senior paramedic in charge of a patient's medical care on-scene with a junior partner. That senior paramedic is responsible for the stabilization and treatment of the victim, even if not in command of the scene. In the case of a full-arrest, the paramedic is securing an airway, delivering cardiac medicine, and making transport decisions. In this situation, the paramedic is functioning as a leader, taking on all the responsibilities and ramifications that come with that role.

To re-emphasize, the fire and emergency services industry operates on leadership at all levels. Moreover, because you are a fire and emergency services professional, you are placed in a leadership position within society, one whom others call upon to render aid—to assist, to save, to lead. The average citizen cannot distinguish the experience or rank of a firefighter or emergency professional. They see a uniform and a badge; they see a professional. Most importantly, they see a *leader*, one who can be depended on and called upon in a time of need, one they trust without question with their possessions, life, or the life of a loved one.

Leadership in Emergencies and Non-Emergencies

This book is not about on-scene command and control. Top-down, centralized management governs an emergency scene, where the on-scene commander is in charge. Orders are given, often in an autocratic manner, and followers carry them out.[6] On-scene command and control operates this way in order to maintain what the pros call scene-cohesiveness and, most of all, scene-safety. All well and good, except when this manner carries over to the day-to-day non-emergency operations and functions, where what should be leadership is in fact *management.*[7] Classical management is about process; it is based upon outcomes and void of relationships; it is spreadsheets and statistics, budgets and staffing. The management process is important to the overall operations and continuity of an organization; however, people, are not processes. They are not the bottom line or end results; they are people. *People* make up the fire and emergency services.

Leaders in the fire and emergency services operate primarily as managers, even in times when they need to operate as leaders.[8] That is not surprising, since most fire and emergency services texts address management practices in-depth and, at most, just scratch the surface on leadership.[9] Textbooks for officers in the profession teach how to budget or staff a station, yet ignore the very essence of the profession, the leading of people and the human element. For example:

> A firefighter comes to your office after returning from an emergency medical services call where a vehicle struck a teenager while in a crosswalk; the seemingly bothered firefighter asked for the night off. The firefighter functioned as the patient technician on this incident; he provided advanced emergency medical care at the scene and en-route to a trauma center. During transport, the patient went into cardiac arrest; everything was done properly to save his life yet the patient died. While the firefighter stood in front of your desk, you pulled out the days staffing roster and said, "We just don't have the staffing and downtown is giving too much grief about using overtime." In this case, you used numbers, a policy, and a spreadsheet to make a decision. You ignored the fact that this firefighter has an adult son you have met who was disabled in an accident when a teenager. During this interaction, you functioned successfully as a bureaucrat, you did everything right according to officer textbooks; however, you missed an opportunity to be a true leader.

This scenario shows how, functioning in a day-to-day management process as if on-scene or concentrating on a bottom line, the fire and emergency services hurts it most precious resource, its people. Sociologist C. Wright Mills referred to this as the bureaucratic ethos.[10] For a vast majority of fire and emergency services organizations, this hierarchical, top down, bureaucratic model of leadership is the norm.[11] Bureaucrats, according to Mills, "are among the humanistically impoverished, living with reference to values that exclude any arising from a respect for human reason."[12] The bureaucrat in the fire and emergency services concentrates on the management process and by doing so places the humanity of followers at arms-length. Bureaucracy allows the manager to avoid making decisions. The bureaucratic process is full of policies and procedures, allowing managers to disown the responsibility that comes from making real decisions. One can act within the policy, blame the policy, and therefore hide behind the policy. Does any of this sound familiar?

> Amanda, one of your rescue technicians, arrives late to a shift, because on her way to work, she stopped at the scene of a rollover and rendered aid until emergency crews arrived. As she enters the station, you as her officer confront her and recite almost verbatim the department's "late" policy. Not allowing her to explain the situation, you tell her if she is late again, she will receive a written reprimand in her file.

The bureaucracy in the fire and emergency services is a cycle populated by good people who never desired to be bureaucrats yet became bureaucrats because, when it comes to leadership, that is the only model they know. One researcher argued that, "many leaders do not study leadership theories, but come to their own style that derives from their learned way of being in the world."[13] If the bureaucratic cycle is to be broken and replaced by leadership, the field needs further education on leadership, not management. We already have plenty of management training. In the case of the rescue technician, a simple "Why are you late?" would have sufficed, then a "Well done!" after she explained her reason. Bureaucrats are incapable of such a response; they rely on policy and procedure as their guide. This, however, does not have to be common practice in the fire and emergency services future.

The "leadership" education that most fire and emergency services professionals currently receive, such as the National Incident Management System and other officer/command certifications, are void of leadership theory and are instead filled with managerial practices and bureaucratic models.[14] Leadership is unlike management because it is not focused on process but on *being*. The leaders we need understand the spreadsheets and discipline policies that are the province of managers, but go beyond them to matters of identity. This cannot be overstated. The kind of leader you are is a direct reflection of *who* you are; your approach toward leadership directly reflects your attitude and thus happiness.[15] Your leadership style is how you approach people; it represents your value system and the virtues you hold dear, placed front-and-center for all to see.

This is what this book is about: introducing a practical leadership approach to the fire and emergency services that goes hand-in-hand with the values of the fire and emergency services.[16] My purpose is to introduce the reader to the philosophy of *servant leadership* by addressing the commonalities between the philosophy's constructs and the fire and emergency services.[17] By addressing these similarities, fire and emergency services professionals can see a leadership philosophy that seems to hold the same values as the profession, with the hopes of making the practice of servant leadership commonplace in the future.

The philosophy of servant leadership is explained here through a fire and emergency services lens. The lack of leadership education and training is a deep-seated problem throughout the fire and emergency services career field, which means by developing texts that speak to the profession, capable professionals who are promoted to leadership positions will not need to scramble to understand the basics of leadership through non-emergency service texts.[18]

This text is **not about teaching you *how* to lead** but, rather, teaching you about a leadership approach that resonates with what it means to be a fire and emergency services responder. It is an arrogant, impossible claim to say that a leadership book can create leaders, because leadership is about one's being; it is about *who you desire to be.* In my own career, I have learned that a book can inform and educate, and it can motivate and help construct a foundation to build one's being as a leader. The individual reader, however, must decide the type of leader he or she desires to be and be willing to spend a lifetime cultivating and tending to leadership abilities through education, self-reflection, and practice.

One significant benefit of servant leadership is that it resonates with those who serve. In my experience, people who are drawn to fire and emergency services careers do not do so from a desire to be a bureaucrat but, rather, a desire to serve. (Heaven knows they do not do it for the money!) Fire and emergency services professionals have experienced the hardships associated with the profession; they have witnessed human tragedy and loss and are continually asked to put the pieces back together.[19] How can such a raw reality be led by a manager? The truth is, it cannot. Focusing on processes and outcomes will not build healthy environments. That only happens by focusing on people, serving their needs as they serve others. As one thoughtful leader has noted, the practice of servant leadership holds promise for the fire and emergency services due to its attributes and its commonality to the profession.[20]

Most likely, you already know who you want to be and it is my hope that by the end of this book, you will also know *what type of leader you want to be*. If this book helps you succeed on your journey to become a servant-leader who leads through a desire to serve, you and the fire and emergency services will be better for it.

CHAPTER 2

THE ROOTS OF SERVANT LEADERSHIP

"One thing I know: the only ones among you who will really be happy are those who will have sought and found how to serve."

– Dr. Albert Schweitzer

THIS CHAPTER INTRODUCES A LEADERSHIP PHILOSOPHY CALLED "servant leadership." As you read about its principles and read the next chapter that explains the characteristics of a servant-leader, you will begin to see commonalities between the ideas of servant leadership and the operating principles that guide the fire and emergency services profession. The remaining chapters explain the "seven virtuous constructs" of servant leadership and show how they are perfectly suited to the fire and emergency services, not as a theory, but as an expression of the way things really work.

Servant leadership is an ancient idea that was first given modern expression by businessman, author, and consultant Robert K. Greenleaf (1904-1990). Greenleaf recognized that at its most fundamental level, a leader is simply someone who has followers. By that standard, Hitler was a leader, as were Mussolini and Stalin. But Greenleaf was interested in ethical leadership, which he distinguished by the leader's motives, uses of power, and evolved skills and capacities applied to not only achieve objectives but to nurture followers along the way.

Greenleaf's core idea is that the true leader is one who seeks to serve first. Here is how he put it:

> It begins with the natural feeling that one wants to serve, to serve first. Then conscious choice brings one to aspire to lead. [The servant-leader] is sharply different from the person who is leader first, perhaps because of the need to assuage an unusual power drive or to acquire material possessions. For such it will be a later choice to serve after leadership is established. The leader first and the servant first are two extreme types. Between them, there are shadings and blends that are part of the infinite variety of human nature." [1]

In other words, servant leadership differs from all other leadership styles because it begins with a desire to serve, whereas other leadership theories begin from a desire to lead. [2]

By now, you may be saying, "Whoa! That's not realistic. Maybe you're talking about a servant-martyr!" Stay with me here--servant leadership is about service, not servitude. Servant leadership is not ice cream for breakfast and the servant-leader is not a softy. Author Steven Covey once said that servant-leaders are the hardest leaders to work for because of their commitment to people. It is difficult to be a servant-leader because it takes work and energy. [3] The servant-leader is committed to the highest-priority needs and growth of people in the organization, sets standards that followers never knew they could achieve, and holds followers to accountability for meeting those standards. [4] I repeat: Servant-leaders commit to helping their followers achieve excellence and to serving their most important needs along the way. Robert Greenleaf wrote that there is a difference between leaders who are motivated to be a servant first and leaders who are more concerned with being a leader first in order to enjoy all the perks and ego power that comes with the title. That difference "manifests itself in the care taken by the servant-first to make sure that other people's highest priority needs are being served." [5]

Greenleaf wrote that being a servant-leader comes down to three pragmatic questions about outcomes that can be measured.[6] The first is: "Do those who are being served, while they are being served, grow as persons?" In other words, are the people you are leading becoming better people as the result of your leadership? Do your followers grow professionally, intellectually, and spiritually? And is that growth beginning to happen now, not five years down the road?

The second question asks whether those being served "become healthier, wiser, freer, more autonomous, more likely themselves to become servants?" The first part of the question is another way of asking whether followers are empowered. The last part, "more likely themselves to become servants," reminds us of one researcher finding that a majority of leaders have become leaders based upon experiences with other leaders.[7] This suggests that people who are exposed to servant leadership as followers have a better chance of becoming servant-leaders themselves.

The third question reminds us that the decisions we make as leaders have consequences: "What is the effect on the least privileged in society; will he [or she] benefit, or, at least, not be further deprived?" This means that a leader who makes an organizational decision should consider the effect on the least-powerful in the organization. A leader who makes a decision that affects the wider society should ask whether the poor and most vulnerable become worse off; will he benefit, or, at least, will he not be further deprived?"

Let's bring this home. Ask yourself: who really suffers when you as the chief of a fire and emergency services organization downsize staffing or close stations? Is it the affluent and successful or the most vulnerable?

Greenleaf outlined other skills and capacities necessary for servant-leaders to act effectively. Most of them are not taught in business schools or explained in popular books that define leadership in heroic, manipulative terms. Greenleaf's other "big ideas" included:

- Persuasion is the preferred use of power, as opposed to manipulation or coercion
- Deep listening as the premier skill of a servant-leader
- Accessing intuition
- Practicing reflection as a way of making decisions
- Practicing foresight as an ethical demand
- Demanding accountability

Greenleaf says that servant leadership is the way to overcome a toxic leadership environment. Since his servant leadership writings first appeared in 1970, and especially after his influential 1977 book *Servant Leadership: A Journey into the Nature of Legitimate Power and Greatness* was published, the most admired leadership gurus in the country have been unpacking the implications of his ideas. Here is a sampling.

Trust builds positive relationships within an organization. A servant-leader does not demand power or dominate others based on his or her title. Rather, legitimate power is accorded the servant-leader by followers because the servant-leader is trusted. This kind of power is a gift and it must be earned every day. [8]

Credibility is closely related to trust. You cannot fake credibility. It, too, is earned by keeping agreements and is based on a life committed to ethical values. A person who is credible to followers is, by definition, one who believes in service and recognizes a power higher than self. [9]

Servant leadership starts "in here," not "out there." Unlike other leadership theories that begin with a desire to lead, servant leadership stems from an inner desire to serve, and a conscious choice to act on that desire. It is, in fact, a way of leading an overall life of service-living, of being at peace with that choice by experiencing a harmony between the internal desire to be a great leader and the external leadership behaviors that flow from that desire. [10] These and other aspects of Greenleaf's thinking have been summarized and expanded upon by other thoughtful leaders, including Larry Spears, whose list of "Ten Characteristics of a Servant-Leader" is explained in the next chapter. For now, here are a few other insights about the servant-leader life as shared by top researchers, authors, and wise servant leadership practitioners.

- Many who choose the path of servant leadership attempt to become the leader they wished they had had in their own careers. [11]
- A servant-leader is a leader who inspires. [12]
- A servant-leader is one who is trusted by others. [13]
- The servant-leader way of operating stems from a desire to serve and an understanding that an organization is only as good as its people; that in order for its people to be good, they must be served. [14]
- A servant-leader strives to live one's life the same as one leads, as an ethical servant to others. [15]
- In public and private life, the servant-leader clings to his or her values and is unwilling to compromise those values because they are one's North Star guiding principles. [16]

Robert Greenleaf stressed that acting as a servant-leader is a conscious choice. You can say that every leader makes a choice to lead in the way he or she prefers, but the fact is, all too often the choice is not fully conscious. A majority of leaders reflect the influence of other leaders, many of whom were probably not focused on the "highest priority needs of others." Stephen Covey noted that this heightened awareness of choosing how to lead as a servant was unique among leadership models. [17]

The choice to be a servant-leader is far-reaching in its implications. It means one will strive to live life by following ethical, congruent values and behaviors. [18] The servant-leader measures actions by an informed conscience and understands that there are repercussions to all they do. Renowned servant leadership scholar Dr. Ann McGee-Cooper calls this a life of service-living. [19]

The issue of trust will be explored further in a later chapter, but it bears mentioning here because Greenleaf wrote that trust is everything. [20] In order to build positive relationships within an organization, a servant-leader must first build trust. [21] Trust cannot be demanded; it must be earned. Trust makes it possible for colleagues to bestow power as a gift, not in response to a demand from a leader who wishes to dominate others. [22] This gift can make great things happen, but it can only come to those whose actions are credible and who have demonstrated a belief in service that transcends personal ego. [23]

Trust builds credibility. There is an old saying among actors that the hardest task is to fake sincerity. That is as true in life as it is on the stage. The inability to fake sincerity and credibility over the long term gives credibility its power because a life committed to ethical values builds credibility. [24]

You now have a solid introduction to servant leadership and are ready to learn about the ten characteristics and seven constructs as they apply to the fire and emergency services. As the book progresses, you will notice an overlap of some of the values and principles discussed. That is because they are all related and they all revolve around the core value of service. Service, in turn, depends on a mature attitude recognizing the relatedness of work, colleagues, and the wider community in a matrix that transcends the self.

As you begin to understand and apply servant leadership, you will find that it is a coherent philosophy of leading and living. It goes beyond the "tips and techniques" of leading; it does not offer bullet points to make you a servant-leader by checking off each item on the list. What it does do is reflect the soulfulness and paradox of authentic human experience and calls forth the best you have to offer as a leader and a person of character.

CHAPTER 3

THE CHARACTERISTICS OF SERVANT LEADERSHIP

"The firefighters' leadership, bravery and technical knowledge are tested on an everyday basis … They cannot hide behind rank, a desk or e-mail."

– John Salka

AFTER STUDYING THE ROOTS OF SERVANT LEADERSHIP, LARRY Spears, former CEO of the Robert K. Greenleaf Center for Servant Leadership and a thoughtful student of Greenleaf's writings, outlined the ten characteristics of the servant-leader.[1] This chapter builds upon the historical development of the question *What is servant leadership?* to delineate and expand upon specific characteristics of a servant-leader, as put forth by Spears, illustrating them from a fire and emergency services perspective.

Spears' ten characteristics took servant leadership from a theory to a usable and identifiable model. His contribution was to define specific and measurable characteristics to identify servant leadership qualities within individual leaders.

Derived from an interpretation of Greenleaf's original essay, *The Servant as Leader*, the characteristics are listening, empathy, healing, awareness, persuasion, conceptualization, foresight, stewardship, commitment to the growth of people, and building community. Specific and yet not exhaustive, these ten characteristics are the *modus operandi* for describing and measuring the servant-leader. They also function as a way to look inward to one's own leadership characteristics.

Listening

The first characteristic of a servant-leader is an ability to listen. International consultant and university professor Robert Neuschel described the servant-leader as an individual others wish to follow, a leader who is open to hearing the concerns of the people and respecting that every individual possesses specific needs and wishes.[3] Spears argued that such an individual is one who possesses the ability and the desire to listen.[4] According to author Stephen Covey, this willingness to listen to others means the leader is conscious of the individual needs of people and thus desires to hear from them.[5]

For the servant-leader, listening is more than hearing direct verbal conversations. It also means hearing and understanding things not said. Dr. Covey believed the act of listening needed to occur absent from the listener thinking about what he or she desired to say next, and that listening also involved the practice of listening internally, thus knowing oneself. For it is in the act of listening that the leader truly leads.[6]

Authors Asbjörnson and Brenner believed that listening is an art, a thing of beauty to behold, which when done right, could create great things. Deep listening allows leaders to hear the speaker's need and truth.[7] Listening allows for the understanding of the underlying causes of struggle and pain. Furthermore, it is only through listening to individuals that the leader can truly lead.

For the fire and emergency services leader, this is about *hearing one's people*. Listening to one's people has nothing to do with noise but everything to do with paying attention to body language, actions, and other non-verbal clues. This kind of listening is hearing between the lines, hearing the things not being said or avoided. Here is an example:

> Several weeks ago, two firefighter-paramedics who serve as medics with the city's S.W.A.T team responded as part of an initial entry team to serve a warrant. During the operation, a teenage girl in the house was shot and killed in crossfire after the team entered the building and was met with gunfire from a male occupant. During the past few shifts, you as shift captain notice that one of the paramedics is not acting right; he is not sleeping, nor is he eating with the other crewmembers in the station, and he's making off-colored, cold remarks when sitting around and someone asks about the call. This is not normal behavior for him; he is usually good-natured and happy.

> In this case, you are hearing what is not being said by this firefighter-paramedic; you are actively listening. In doing so, you can talk to him in private. You can get him counseling to deal with the trauma of the situation and talk about it instead of bottling it up. You also see the need to talk to his partner, the other firefighter-paramedic on the call, and not just for information on his teammate but to determine his state of health, as well. If the situation is affecting one, there is a strong possibility that it is affecting both.

For the fire and emergency services leader, the act of listening to one's inner voice is as important for one's health as for survival. As a trained professional, you know when something is not right. Over time, experiences and training leave lasting mental impressions. One must listen to these impressions; they can predict what will happen next and may save not only the life of a crew you command, but your own, as well! This is the leader's internal voice; it is constantly speaking and needs to be heard.

Listening to those you serve is also vital. What are they saying and what are they not telling you directly? Is there something you are missing? Fire and emergency services responders encounter this challenge daily in domestic violence, abuse, drug-related, and mental health responses. Do you see abnormal bruises? Is a child acting guarded or appearing frightened of someone else on-scene? Do you continually answer calls from a female exhibiting trauma who seems to always be "falling"? This is what you hear when you actively listen, when you are not seeking specifics, but rather are listening to the scene, listening to those you serve.

Empathy

The second characteristic of the servant-leader is related to listening without judgment: empathy. An empathic leader desires to understand another person's needs, wants, personality traits, and behaviors that stem from specific life experiences and demographic backgrounds.[8] Ken Blanchard and Ken Hodges concluded that such differences are in fact *assets* and that the constant growth of individuals, which includes their uniqueness, only makes an organization stronger.[9]

Research shows that empathetic feelings and behaviors have some surprising effects. Researchers Ekundayo, Damhoeri, and Ekundayo found that empathy can reduce suffering, enhance the ability to care for those in need, and help one find his or her humanity.[10] Empathy is a driving factor to the enlightenment and overall growth of a leader, and a leader's emotional intelligence improves with the ability to empathize.[11]

For the fire and emergency services responder, the goal is to minimize, reduce, or if possible, stop suffering. This can mean anything from rescuing a cat to saving a life to minimizing damage to property that protects irreplaceable family heirlooms. What Ekundayo et al. wrote about that applies to the servant-leader also goes to the heart of what it means to be a fire and emergency services responder. In the case of protecting family heirlooms, empathy involves seeing the value of priceless possessions not through one's own eyes but rather through the eyes of those one serves. Fire and emergency responders are often called to respond to incidents involving individuals and families of a low socioeconomic level. What one may view at a glance as worthless, broken things may in fact be the only possessions these individuals and families own. To them, these possessions are priceless. For example:

> As a lieutenant of an engine company, you and your crew of firefighters respond to a structure fire in an apartment complex. On arrival, you find one apartment engulfed in flames and the other apartment adjacent to the fire beginning to fill with smoke. You have been to this building before for inspections and emergency medical service calls. You know that African refugee families occupy many of the units. What little these families own, and it is not much, is inside of the structure. You immediately call for salvage operations and more units to respond, expressing your empathy for the situation and for the plight of the least among us in society.

In *The Servant as Leader*, Greenleaf advised leaders to ask this about their leadership practices: What is the effect on the least privileged in society? Will they benefit or at least not be further deprived? "This is what it means to be a fire and emergency services responder. At its core, the profession is about serving and protecting all people, especially those who are the least privileged and most vulnerable in society. As the lieutenant, your actions were an outward showing of your empathy, you had a duty to protect these families; you understood this duty, and in this understanding, you served.

Another aspect of empathy and the fire and emergency services responder involves being able to respond and listen to those in need without judgment. They do not call upon you so that you can sit in judgment of them or take their situation personally. As a fire and emergency services responder, you respond to the community's needs and render aid at the utmost professional level. This can only happen if the responder is able to empathize with those they are called upon to serve. A responder's empathy allows victims and patients to be seen as people.

Healing

The third characteristic of the servant-leader is healing. Spears argued that healing takes place in two specific areas: the healing of one's spirit and the healing of others' spirits. "Spirit" refers to the inner self or inner being. The concept of *spirit* can have religious connotations based on usage or situation, but the idea of healing one's spirit in the context of servant leadership is not specific to a single religion, faith, or belief.

Dr. Robert Spitzer, a Jesuit and scholar, wrote that evoking one's spirit strengthens the ability to lead and that the desire to serve stems directly from the spirit or inner self.[12] Integrating spirit, service, and leadership balances one's entire life, because the actions, morals, and ethics expressed by the leader in his or her professional environment need to exist in the leader's personal life, as well.[13]

This is literally true in the public's mind. The hats and t-shirts worn by fire and emergency services professionals stand out as billboards, as advertisements of their organization. When worn off-duty in public, responders are obligated to responsibly represent that honorable image. Their actions represent the organization; when they are judged, the organization is judged. The individual and the organization are one and the same. Furthermore, the individual represents an entire profession.

Healing of one's self builds upon the idea that the servant-leader's approach can be a spiritual one, deriving from a belief in something larger than self.[14] Larry Spears discussed the notion of broken souls in need of repair, a process that is important because the desire to be a servant-leader exists in one's self and soul. Therefore, at the heart of spiritual healing is ultimately the healing of one's self, for as one strives to heal others, the healer is healed as well.[15] Furthermore, at the core of spiritual healing is the forgiveness of others and self.[16]

The fire and emergency services constantly battle tragedy and loss, including both victims they respond to and fellow responders. Each loss taxes the psyche of the responder.[17] The fire and emergency services responder is left questioning humanity itself, playing witness to what humans are capable of doing and the losses people must endure. They mentally return to the occurrence, wondering if they missed something or made the wrong decision. When a line-of-duty death occurs, on-scene commanders are left to question the order they gave; over and over, they ask themselves whether they made the right call, whether their decision cost the lives of responders. This is why healing is so important to the career field. Humans, regardless of ability, are mentally fragile, the macho image and indestructible attitude that accompany the fire and emergency services responder is a façade.[18] For responders to go on, they need to receive healing and need to be able to forgive themselves.

Again, the premise of fire and emergency response is to render aid and assistance to those in need. Healing others is part of this role. The responders' actions toward those they serve reflect their inner desire to heal others and to make the situation better. The nobility of this benevolent commitment is that it is free of ulterior motives—responders simply desire to heal those in need any way they can.

Dr. Earl Braxton, who helps executives and organizations address their dysfunctions, calls for the practice of healing to come into the organization in order to bring it back from turmoil.[19] His argument is that individuals within an organization can never go forward unless the healing process is cultivated and supported. In other words, healing must occur for an organization and its individuals to be whole.

Fire and emergency services organizations, like all others, see their share of troubled times. Fraud, corruption, staffing cuts, and promotions can all have negative impacts. The leader's role is to unite the organization and heal its wounds. This is vital to the individuals who serve and to the overall future of the organization.

Awareness

The fourth characteristic of the servant-leader is awareness. According to Greenleaf, "Awareness is not a giver of solace; it is just the opposite. It is a distributer and an awakener. Able leaders are usually sharply awake and reasonable disturbed."[20] This form of awareness includes an awareness of self and one's own abilities, strengths, and weaknesses, as well as a keen situational awareness.[21] Heightened awareness keeps the fire and emergency services responder from becoming complacent. Moreover, awareness keeps the fire and emergency services leader alert and in a constant state of concern for others, as well as in a constant state of evaluation of the organization. On-scene awareness relates directly to the leader's ability to make calculated, intelligent decisions.

Greenleaf wrote that being aware strengthens one's ability to function within a particular situation and understand relevant needs, both now and in the future. In other words, a leader should have awareness of the current situation, the people who are present, and the path the situation is likely to follow. A leader also needs awareness of the abilities of all who are involved in the situation, including the leader.[22]

On the emergency scene, this awareness drives a constant state of sizing-up, communicating with crews, realizing conditions, and making changes accordingly. Awareness overcomes complacency and drives pride in decision-making.[23] In the midst of the action, awareness means being alert to needs and changing conditions, knowing crew assignments, scene progress, and where, specifically, different operations are taking place.

Educator and researcher Dr. Mary Jensen argued that there needs to be an awareness of self in order for the leader to lead successfully[24]. For the fire and emergency services leader, this translates into awareness of personal abilities, personal strengths and weaknesses. For the responder, this means being aware of one's limitations, part of which means knowing what you are trained and certified to do versus what your pride wants you to do. This can be difficult for both the leader and follower; it is hard for the fire and emergency services responder, regardless of rank, to admit limitations.[25]

Persuasion

Spears identified the ability to persuade as the fifth characteristic of the servant leader. Greenleaf contrasted persuasion with the more usual ways of influencing others—coercion and manipulation. In fact, persuasion stems from one's ability to influence without needing to intimidate.[26] Persuasion takes more time because the goal is not to beat down others with arguments until they comply, but to assist them in embracing the rightness of a position so they accept it for themselves. This is all done in the context of the persuader being open to changing positions, too. The good news is that persuasion grows over time, from one influenced person to the next, and persistence drives persuasion.[27]

For the fire and emergency services, persuasion is the antithesis of autocratic rule. It is the opposite of bully-management. Persuasion involves influencing others by your actions and ideas instead of the practice of *because-I-said-so*.

The power to persuade comes from being trusted. When followers trust their leader, when they see their leader has integrity and is loyal to them, persuasion becomes a natural process. Furthermore, when followers accept a leader's vision, they trust his or her decisions and thus easily come around to a leader's ideas.[28] For the fire and emergency services leader, persuasion comes naturally with orders given. The leader can make decisions and give orders that are followed, not because of rank but rather trust. The leader's integrity and ability persuades others to want to follow.

Persuasion is an anti-authority trait that stems from an individual's ability, not specifically his or her position of power.[29] However, such a trait does not mean that the actual leader relinquishes his or her position of responsibility.[30] Rather, the servant-leader is one who views leadership as decentralized, a shared authority of all those involved.[31] This has a place in both emergency scene operations and day-to-day operations of the organization. A leader can persuade others to want to strive for a certain vision or certification level across the organization. Servant-leaders, without having to stand over their followers, can have a vision carried out without question. Their people are empowered and thus persuaded to want to go in a specific direction. For instance:

> A fire chief at an International Airport desired to pursue accreditation through the Center of Public Safety Excellence, a process of self-assessment that takes years of hard work. The fire chief knew the benefits of being accredited, as well as the daunting task of undergoing the process. She oversaw three stations on the airport and 250 personnel. The fire chief had two options:; she could order her followers to take on the task of accreditation or she could persuade them to want to take on the task. Knowing how much work was involved in the process, the chief decided to persuade her members.

> As fire chief, she was trusted and well liked throughout the organization. She had made decisions in the past that had benefited the organization and its members; and, because of that, she was able to persuade her followers to want to help with a process that required them to contribute more than their already established responsibilities.

This ability to influence others to follow a new path, to work for and accept change, comes from being able to persuade, and that ability shows in successful leadership outcomes.[32] Furthermore, persuasion allows success to occur without authoritative behavior. Leaders can bring their ideas and desires to fruition without coercion, as in the case of the airport fire chief.

Conceptualization

Spears identified the ability to conceptualize as the sixth characteristic of the servant leader. Greenleaf discussed the ability to conceptualize not as a characteristic, but as a talent or a gift.[33] Conceptualization involves the ability to envision the big picture, using historical information of the past in order to understand the need in the present. The leader who possesses the ability to conceptualize is in fact a visionary.[34] A visionary committed to continuous ongoing vision is not satisfied with the status quo, nor supportive of a stagnant atmosphere.[35]

Within the fire and emergency services organization, the status quo holds dangers. Refusing to change or take on new responsibilities can lead to issues involving staffing reductions, station closings, and contracting out services to another organization, to name just a few hazards. The conceptualizing leader can understand the big picture of both the organization and the community being served, envision the needs of followers and citizens, and offer a continuous vision of better, more effective service delivery.

More specifically, the fire and emergency services leader has the responsibility to conceptualize:

- station staffing
- resource allocation
- operations based upon a changing environment
- training and readiness

- worst-case scenarios
- the one-in-a-million chance calls

The leader then needs to be able to develop mitigation and prevention plans, all the while carrying out and overseeing the daily activities that take up the bulk of most fire and emergency services organizations' time.

The ability to conceptualize for tomorrow is not easy while expending time to lead for today. That's why Greenleaf calls it a talent. Australian researchers Sen Sendjaya and André Pekerti wrote that the very idea of servant leadership was a conceptualized vision of Greenleaf's.[36] However, the dreamer, or in the case of the servant-leader, the visionary, needs to harness his or her visions and bring them into reality.[37]

Foresight

Spears identified foresight as the seventh characteristic of the servant leader. Foresight is directly related to conceptualization; the two go hand-in-hand to form a leader's ability to vision. Greenleaf wrote that foresight is a central tenet of servant leadership and is an *ethical* duty of a leader, because a lot of damage can ensue if a leader fails to understand likely scenarios.

What is foresight? Greenleaf said it is not about being able to see the future like a psychic, but "is a better than average guess about what is going to happen [and] when in the future."[38] And how do we develop the ability to envision a likely future? It starts with learning, through both reading and life experiences. Ken Blanchard puts it succinctly: "Since organizations are being bombarded with change, you would be wise to make learning a top priority and constantly strive to adapt to new circumstances."[39] Learning helps a leader develop the ability to sense patterns and to predict trends and needs going forward, based upon prior understandings of knowledge, critical thinking, and reflection.

The fire and emergency services profession is not exempt from a world where factors affecting technology, building construction, population, and social structures are ever evolving. A fire and emergency services leader who is status quo oriented and devoid of foresight fails as a leader for a very simple reason: response priorities and capabilities can be compromised when they are needed most.[40]

For example, a fire chief leading Aircraft Rescue Fire Fighting (ARFF) services may face future aircraft emergencies with aircraft capable of carrying over 600 passengers. These numbers change the dynamics of professional tasks, which means that the ARFF chief officer who waits to prepare may be responsible for catastrophic losses.

Again, a leader who practices foresight studies history, understands the present, and can conceptualize and envision a future that takes into account the needs and direction of an organization and its people.[41] This ability is not only a testament to a leader's intelligence, but also to wisdom, and it is a serious matter.[42] A lack of foresight greatly increases the chance that a leader is destined to fail, and a leader who lacks the ability to see future needs and directions is doomed from the start.[43] Furthermore, other researchers have agreed with Greenleaf that the failure to foresee future needs and trends is an ethical issue, which ultimately leads to a leader's demise, and that foresight stems from thinking about the whole and not simply a part.[44]

In the case of the fire and emergency services, the demise associated with a lack of foresight is ultimately to the detriment of followers and the community at large. The fire and emergency services is unlike other fields. The decisions, actions, and inactions associated with the profession have a direct effect on human life and suffering. Therefore, a failure of foresight pertaining to emergency planning, prevention, and responses is an unacceptable failure of leadership. A leader who is only reactive after a disaster is already too late.

Stewardship

Stewardship is the eighth characteristic of the servant-leader. In medieval times, a steward was the "keeper of the hall" who had a mandate to administer the lord's estate in all matters large and small. The steward might delegate, but was personally accountable for everything that happened in the entire estate. Put another way, the steward was charged with the greater good of the estate.

That role is parallel to the meaning of stewardship for a servant-leader. The good steward-leader is charged with seeing to the greater good.[45]

Stewardship requires one to vision things as a whole rather than consider each issue as an isolated entity void of connections to other issues.[46] For fire and emergency services leaders, the *whole* is the followers and the community that they serve. This is the sum of the parts, the great responsibility that is bigger than leaders themselves. When an individual accepts the rank of a fire and emergency services leader, he or she is accepting a responsibility that carries with it *total service* to followers and community.

A good steward not only seeks the greatest good, but also seeks meaning.[47] Servant-leaders realize that their successes relate to the successes of others. Fire and emergency services leaders are only as good as their followers, for it is their followers that carry out the mission, and they do so in the context of stewardship of the greater good. The fire and emergency services leader as steward is entrusted with a leadership role that includes the responsibility to grow the organization and its members for the betterment of society itself.

Commitment to the Growth of People

The ninth characteristic of the servant-leader is a commitment to the growth of people. This commitment involves a leader's devotion to the success and well-being of each individual. Being committed to the growth of people means the servant-leader fosters an environment where the desire for the individual to succeed flourishes. It means being there for people, caring about their personal struggles, expressing gratitude for their commitment and successes, bringing them into the fold, and nurturing them to be better.[48]

A successful fire and emergency services response is based on education and proper ongoing training. The fire and emergency services leader must be resolutely committed to training and development in order to deliver to the public effective emergency response. This responsibility includes a commitment to each individual's best qualities, meaning the leader must strive to bring out abilities that followers did not know they had. This involves pushing followers to levels they never knew they could reach and not accepting mediocrity in their performance.

Ken Blanchard and Ken Hodges argue that commitment to the growth of people involves viewing people as appreciating assets and not just temporary solutions.[49] When leaders view their followers as appreciating assets, they cultivate and serve them, knowing that the time spent in service will produce great rewards. Fire and emergency services leaders who spend time cultivating their human assets produce effective emergency responders capable of dealing with any situation they may face. Furthermore, because the power of servant leadership lies within the individual, a servant-leader who fosters individual growth is in fact nurturing future servant-leaders.

Building Community

The tenth and final characteristic of the servant-leader is building community within an organization. The fire and emergency services functions as a community and the very essence of the profession is teamwork. Several researchers have argued that servant leadership strengthens community between people far better than other leadership styles.[50] This ability to foster and sustain community is so important that Greenleaf states, "Where there is not community, trust, and respect, ethical behavior is difficult for the young to learn and for the old to maintain."[51] The process of building community brings individuals together to form a whole.[52] That, in turn, strengthens the organization for the greater good.[53]

The profession operates as a community of responders.[54] This community is made up of individuals served by their leaders and entrusted to carry out grueling and often dangerous work. The strength of the community within the fire and emergency services is the effectiveness of its teams, and the effectiveness of its teams hinges on the leaders who effectively serve them.[55]

As shown in this chapter, a servant-leader within the fire and emergency services can not only build community but can also provide other leadership qualities that strengthen the noble mission: listen deeply, express genuine empathy, nurture healing, operate with high awareness, use persuasion rather than coercion and manipulation, take the time for conceptualization, practice foresight and stewardship, and demonstrate commitment to the growth of people. The following chapter will discuss the history and specific leadership challenges of a fire and emergency services leader.

CHAPTER 4

THE CONSTRUCTS OF SERVANT LEADERSHIP
AND THE FIRE AND EMERGENCY SERVICES

"I can think of no more stirring symbol of man's humanity to man than a fire engine."

– *Kurt Vonnegut*

THE HISTORY OF THE FIRE AND EMERGENCY SERVICES DATE BACK millennia. The Egyptians invented a water pump in the third century B.C. and the Romans were the first to organize fire-fighting efforts. Major catastrophes like the 1666 London fire changed cities and landscapes and sparked the creation of professional fire and emergency response organizations.[1] The people who were called upon to deal with the unique situations were called *firemen* and then, over time, became known as *firefighters*. Today, a firefighter is a fire and emergency services professional, taking on expanded roles in emergency medical services, hazardous materials, and all-hazard responses.[2] Today's fire and emergency services professional still holds true to the same passions and traditions as those who came before, based on love for the profession and a desire to serve others.[3]

Fire and emergency services responders, unlike the vast majority of firemen in the past, earn advanced certifications in technical rescue, paramedic, hazardous materials, officer levels, and aircraft rescue firefighting. Furthermore, a vast majority of fire and emergency services professionals hold undergraduate and graduate degrees, many at the time of hire. Even though the industry still operates as a para-military organization, the fire and emergency services has moved slowly from a blue-collar job to a white-collar career driven by education, responsibility, and salary. The fire and emergency services must acknowledge this evolution and abandon the shop-floor culture that feeds certain poor leadership practices, adopting a more professional approach toward leadership.[4]

What has not changed about the profession is the fact that it still plays witness to the tragedies of others. Invited into the lives of strangers, the responder enters, without question, into chaos and suffering while shouldering the burdens associated with being responsible for putting another's world back together. Because of this role, it is assumed the responder is macho, concrete, and unaffected. The very fact that responders enter this profession makes them seemingly fearless and emotionally healthy.[5] In truth, many responders do feel this way. Because of their chosen profession and the fact that they are well-trained and brave, many responders assume they are invincible, immune to the psychological and emotional effects that come from emergency incidents.[6]

However, this is not the case; it is just the opposite. Responders are vulnerable to powerful psychological blowback even if they do not realize it, or worse, they do not *want* to realize it.[7] The responder not only must deal with the physical loss of property, but the psychological impact of not being able to save a life or live with an order or deal with a possible oversight that led to a responder being injured or killed.[8] The masculine mythology of the profession drives a belief that as the helper, one cannot ask for help, and thus, many fire and emergency responders are taking their own lives in a last-ditch effort to try to find peace within a bureau-cracy tasked with mitigating even the smallest chaos.[10]

This reality creates a great balancing act for fire and emergency services leaders. In their role as officers, they are tasked with command and control, the management of an *organization,* or part thereof, as well as leading *people.* They must function as autocratic managers on an emergency scene, managers of organizations, and leaders of men and women living in close-knit family-like conditions. The first leadership role associated with on-scene emergency management involves a direct, authoritative role, giving commands and orders to crews.[11] In this role, the fire and emergency services officer has clear-cut directives and procedures to follow, and they understand the position and the responsibilities associated with it. Directing crews, coordinating operations, and making decisions on-scene, though mentally taxing, are straightforward tasks.

The second leadership role, management of the organization, is, again, straightforward. Fire and emergency services organizations have policies and procedures regarding day-to-day operations. In this role, management mimics paint-by-numbers.

For example, you must staff a paramedic rescue unit daily at station three in a department that has 24-hour rotating shifts comprised of three groups, "A," "B," and "C." If the policy calls for three-handed paramedic rescues and all three positions require a paramedic certification, then three paramedics are assigned to rescue at station three, on "A" group, "B" group, and "C" group, for their 24-hour shifts. If a vacancy or leave issue arises, you fill the vacancy following the established staffing policy. In this case, the management function is clear-cut.

The leadership role, however, is far different away from the emergency scene and the daily management of the organization. In this situation, leadership involves all of the dynamics that leaders face in any other organization, especially the challenges of human relationships.[12] This leadership role is not clear-cut; no policies are in place for dealing with emotions or the growth of individuals. You will find no directives to guide the officer on how to empower people or build community within the organization. Hence, the purpose of this book: to bring together a leadership approach that relates directly to the core of why individuals choose a career in the fire and emergency services—a desire to serve.[13]

Until now, literature about leadership practices has long ignored the fire and emergency services.[14] At best, they have brushed over the topic of leadership and instead focused on administrative functions.[15] Again, administrative and management functions are vital to an organization's operation; however, by not providing leadership texts and education written specifically for the fire and emergency services, the profession is hurting its people.[16]

A Word about Constructs

The majority of this book is based on what are called "constructs of servant leadership." The normal meaning of the word *construct* is to build something, and the word is used as a verb. In the world of academia and theoretical science, however, *construct* is often used as a noun, and it refers to a model that is built systematically from other ideas. Think of it as a blueprint. In the context that the word is used here, a *construct* can also refer to the individual ideas that are combined to explain the whole.

Greenleaf's explanation of the motive of the servant as leader—the desire to serve—is the same driving force that brings people to the fire and emergency services profession. The goal of this book is to put forth a pragmatic leadership approach that resonates with the motives of fire and emergency services professionals by using the constructs of servant leadership, which run parallel to what it means to be a fire and emergency services responder.

Because Greenleaf's ideas are such a rich source of inspiration, a number of researchers have tried their hand at summarizing servant leadership principles for different disciplines. The constructs of servant leadership described here were distilled by Dr. Kathleen Patterson from Greenleaf's 1970 seminal essay *The Servant as Leader*.[17] Patterson argued that servant leadership extended beyond the transformational leadership model, one that is mentioned in certain fire and emergency services administrative texts, and therefore demanded its own set of parameters; thus, the seven constructs specific to servant leadership. Patterson and her colleagues argued that without concrete concepts identified as specific to servant leadership, true empirical research, and thus understanding, could not occur.[18] Even though similarities exist between the theory of transformational leadership and servant leadership, certain foundational aspects cause the two theories to be completely different from one another.[19] The core difference between the two theories is how one arrives at leadership, either from a desire to lead or a desire to serve.[20] This difference strengthens the argument that servant leadership theory fits within the fire and emergency services profession, because the fire and emergency services responder arrives at the profession from a desire to serve.

In order, Patterson's constructs are *agapao* love, humility, altruism, vision, trust, empowerment, and service. Her research shows how each construct flows into the next, leading to the final construct of service. The next seven chapters explain each of Patterson's seven constructs and show how each relates to the fire and emergency services. Each chapter is written in a way as to spark critical thinking and reflection about their fit within the fire and emergency services.

Remember that becoming a servant-leader is not about major organizational change, but rather, a change in approach and attitude.[21]

CHAPTER 5

AGAPAO LOVE

"I don't necessarily have to like my players and associates but as their leader, I must love them. Love is loyalty, love is teamwork, love respects the dignity of the individual. This is the strength of any organization."

  – *Vince Lombardi*

THE FIRST OF PATTERSON'S SEVEN VIRTUOUS CONSTRUCTS OF servant leadership is *agapao* love. In this sense, love is at the core of authentic leadership, an unwavering moral and ethical commitment to others.[1] A servant-leader is formed by *agapao* love, which exists simultaneously with one's desire to serve. The love and desire are, in essence, one and the same.

Love overcomes fear and hostilities within organizations and drives away negativity.[2] It is love that cements a commitment to one's followers and a desire to see them succeed.[3] Love given from leader to follower is the energy that drives success and creativity.[4] Love is more than emotion; it also includes understanding and appreciation.[5]

Within the fire and emergency services, there is an expectation that those who serve *shall* succeed. Unlike other professions, failure within the fire and emergency services can lead to tragedy. Such pressures, at times, have a negative impact on the responder.[6] For the fire and emergency services leader, it is imperative to understand this issue and, out of love, to *lead.* We have learned that the fire and emergency services responder is vulnerable to the same psychological issues that civilians face.[7] Thus, for fire and emergency services responders to succeed, they also need to *be* loved, not only to do their jobs, but also to recover from their jobs.

To understand this point, one needs look no further than a shooting at a Newtown, Connecticut, elementary school. In this incident, local fire and emergency services, unaware of the carnage, responded to a scene where 20 children and six teachers were assassinated in an elementary school. The victims, most of whom were between the ages of six and seven, were killed by an assailant armed with an assault rifle. The responders played witness to this evil act as they entered into a scene that would change their worlds forever. Imagine the emotions of responders in turnout and SWAT gear as they responded to a scene where their skills were little to no use, hoping for a chance to make the situation just a little better, but left with a feeling of helplessness.

This is an example of a situation where it is imperative that fire and emergency services responders receive love from both their leaders and colleagues. In this incident, responders left to journey alone found themselves trying to survive.[8] Effective leadership in highly emotional cases involves listening and supporting followers, letting them know they are cared for and not alone.[9] The research is in, and it shows that love begins the healing process, as trite as that may sound.

In his book *Leadership and the Force of Love*, Dr. John Hoyle wrote that a leader who cannot love is incapable of true leadership.[10] In fact, Dr. Hoyle and his colleague Dr. Robert Slater argue that love's power is the *most* reliable way to overcome destructive practices within organizations.

And what does love really look like in the context of leadership? It is not a mushy, abstract ideal, but an expression communicated through actions that are authentic, unselfish, and taken from a moral base. We are not talking about the gestures of puppy love, but mature, thoughtful behavior that is done without the expectation of receiving anything in return. The role of a leader should be a daunting yet enjoyable experience, both "out there" in the world, and "in here," where one finds deep happiness.[12] Stephen Covey argues that love is the foundation of happiness.[13] Celebrated poet and author James Autry agrees that happiness as a leader comes not only from professional success, but from the love and esteem one has for colleagues.[14]

Here is another way of putting it: you can learn certain techniques of leadership, but love makes it all worthwhile.

At the close of a series of speeches Robert Greenleaf gave at Dartmouth Alumni College in 1968, he said, "In the end, nothing really counts but love and friendship."[15] The notion of love, at least from the standpoint of servant leadership, stems from the unconditional love that comes from a moral (not moralistic) base.[16] This love is unwavering, possessing a power to conquer fear and establish an authentic leader-follower relationship.[17] One can only derive goodness from love.

The fire and emergency services profession needs all the help it can get in conquering fear. These public servants, regardless of past experiences and human instincts for self-preservation, enter daily into unchartered territory, facing situations that most would rationally flee. If you are a company level leader, you will draw on your love for those entrusted to you to keep them safe. Your abiding concern for their well-being will motivate you to hone your skills, remain aware, and place their safety and security above all else. And when you do that, love is reciprocated. Your followers realize you love them because of the way you look out for them in every situation. That is probably the biggest reason they will willingly place themselves in harm's way without second-guessing your decisions, and will also gift to you the power to teach them.

Let's be honest about something that people who do not work in our profession may not understand: the fire and emergency services profession is inherently a competitive career field. The recruitment process rewards competitiveness. It is not unusual to see only several individuals, sometimes out of thousands of applicants, selected for a recruit-candidate position. The competition doesn't end there, though. Becoming a recruit-candidate means first passing a grueling testing and selection process. Then selected recruit-candidates *might* receive an appointment letter after completing a year or more of probationary training and evaluation. Once appointed, each individual will compete for positions, special schools, and assignments. Furthermore, such competitiveness remains throughout one's entire career, as individuals compete for rank advancement and promotion.[18]

Competition drives success, yet it cannot be allowed to stifle relationships and consume a person's being. There are times when leaders may feel intimidated or threatened by a follower's ability and feel in competition with that follower. What Hoyle and Slater argued is that such competition should never overcome love for one's colleagues, leaders, or followers.[19]

This same love is the reason they can come to you, because they know you have their best interests in mind. Your unconditional acceptance of them as persons allows them to confide in you, professionally and personally.[20] Unlike an arms-length bureaucrat, you are approachable and sought out because of your ability to love. When we lead out of love, we do so because we understand that bureaucracy can hurt people and stifle great leadership practices.[21]

Leadership scholar Dr. Bruce Winston discussed love's power within the context of leadership, arguing that one does not use followers as a means to an end.[22] This means that a leader who leads through love values one's followers for who they are as people. This notion goes against the bureaucracy's model, which consists of multiple layers of process and policy, replacing them instead with the needs of one's people. Let's be even more explicit: within the fire and emergency services, leaders who love their people do not use and abuse them in order to make the next rank.

This, however, does not mean that a leader's love should be mistaken for an anti-disciplinarian attitude, or the leader is seen as a doormat. Instead, *agapao* love allows a leader to render *just* decisions, decisions never made in anger or haste.[23] We can call this tough servant-leader love, taking actions because you are committed to the growth of people. Dr. Ann McGee-Cooper calls accountability "the taproot of servant leadership," which means that bad actions and choices that your followers make cannot be ignored.[24] However, because you love them, your decisions will be for their good, irrespective of personal relationships and regardless of how they perceive it. Your decisions come from the heart.[25] Take a moment and reflect upon the following:

> You are a battalion chief assigned to a fire department's fire prevention and investigation bureau. In your duties, you receive an assignment to investigate a potential crime scene where a small fire took place when the police were attempting to serve a search warrant; you decide to take another lieutenant with you to the scene to assist in the investigation. You have known this lieutenant for over a decade and trained him in arson investigations. The scene is located in a neighborhood drug house, which on arrival, you find littered with small amounts of drugs, some weapons, and cash. The police have the scene cordoned off and vacated the interior so you can do an investigation. During the investigation process, you witness the lieutenant pick up a small-caliber pistol from an end table and put it in his pocket. Making a mental note, you continue your

investigation, take pictures and samples, then clean up your equipment and exit the structure.

When you get back to your office you confront the lieutenant, insist he hand the pistol over to you, and ask him why he stole evidence. He reports to you that he felt it did not matter because the weapon belonged to a drug dealer and nobody would care. You then tell him it does matter, the police care, and that regardless who you steal from, it is wrong. After some time in your office, you inform the lieutenant that you have to bring disciplinary actions against him.

Does this mean that you do not love him? Does this mean that because you love him, you will not allow such a breach of trust to occur? Would allowing the lieutenant's actions to go unpunished be for his own good? Does the lieutenant demonstrate reciprocal love by placing you in such a compromising situation and expecting you to look the other way?

The love of a leader toward followers is neither a weakness, nor a relinquishing of authority, but rather a compassionate practice that brings people together.[26] Rodney Ferris, who has written about the power of love in organizations, argues that the practice of love, seeing the need to be committed both morally and ethically to one's followers, makes a stronger, more effective leader.[27] Placing love at the forefront of leadership makes it far more difficult for unethical practices to take hold.[28] Furthermore, love leads to the desire to serve, and thus to becoming a servant-leader.[29]

People need to feel safe and to feel safe they need to be loved.[30] Therefore, if you *begin* with love, people feel safe.[31] Moreover, people who are loved reciprocate such love through their performance.[32]

All of this talk of love and safety takes on heightened importance on an emergency scene where personal safety cannot be taken for granted. Feeling loved by your comrades and leaders can certainly help you feel safer. It can even save your life.

A leader's desire to want his or her people to succeed stems from love. A loving leader wants to recognize the potential of one's followers and foster their abilities. Love recognizes the importance of people who are successful in their jobs and understands that anything less is harmful to the organization as well as to the individual.[33] Love seeks out the truth and stands on a solid foundation of honesty and openness.[34]

A love for one's fellow man brings people to the fire and emergency services profession allows them to remain.[35] The conscientious decision to enter into the fire and emergency services career field comes with a complete understanding of the inherent dangers associated with the profession.[36] It is a love for serving others in their most vulnerable time of need that, throughout history, has called individuals to the profession.[37] Love, however, also allows one to sacrifice life itself for another. Take, for example, the sacrifice of Firefighter Jon Davies:

> Firefighter Jon Davies of the Worcester Fire Department. Firefighter Davies, a 17-year veteran, was there the day the Worcester Fire Department lost six firefighters at the Cold Storage Warehouse fire. Firefighter Davies arrived on-scene as part of the first alarm complement and stayed on for days working the charred rubble. For several days, he worked to locate the bodies of his fallen brothers and then assisted his fellow members and their families in burying their dead. After this tragedy, Firefighter Davies went back and honorably served the people of Worcester for twelve more years.

> Twelve years to the month after the Worcester Fire Department lost six of its own at the Cold Storage Warehouse fire, tragedy struck again; this time the loss was Firefighter Jon Davies. He was killed during a search and rescue operation at a tenement house while searching for a reported missing tenant.[38] Firefighter Davies' love for his fellow man allowed him to willingly be placed in harm's way, and he ultimately

sacrificed his own life while attempting to save the life of a total stranger.

Regardless of rank and years of service, fire and emergency services professionals are leaders within their communities. By loving their profession, they also love the community they serve. This love, not a salary, motivates the fire and emergency services responders to return to duty after a tragedy.

Greenleaf was right; in the end nothing counts but love and friendship, and *showing* love, caring for one's people, is the key to successful leadership. It's a fact of life: When you love something, you become passionate about it. If you love your people, you become passionate about them. If you are passionate about your people, you become committed to them, and most of all, you desire to serve them.

CHAPTER 6

HUMILITY

"To be humble to superiors is duty, to equals courtesy, to inferiors nobleness."

– *Benjamin Franklin*

HUMILITY IS THE SECOND CONSTRUCT OF SERVANT LEADERSHIP. To be humble does not mean that one relinquishes power or position but, rather, realizes the humanity in both self and others.[1] In an essay that outlines lessons from America's "quiet CEOs," Merwin A. Hayes and Michael D. Comer concluded that "Humility is one of the most important attributes of leadership, because it helps connect the leader to the follower through their common bond of humanity."[2] A humble leader achieves great things yet remains grounded as a person. Researchers Lee Hean and Guat Tin showed that humility in leadership actually *improves* the org nization, a surprising finding to many who think the proper role of a leader is to always be strong, and even sometimes grandiose.[3]

Earlier in this book you learned that competition in the fire and emergency services is normal. There is constant competition to be the fastest, the most accomplished, the strongest, and the fittest. In the recruit academy and beyond, firefighters take part in "bunker-drills." A bunker-drill begins with firefighters standing behind their turnout gear and self-contained breathing apparatus (SCBA) while an officer stands in the center with a stopwatch. On the word Go, the firefighters are timed as they don their turnout gear and SCBA. All departments run bunker-drills and though they are supposedly about being able to put on your gear quickly and correctly, they are, in fact, competitions between firefighters. Not that there is anything wrong with that kind of competition if it hones life-saving skills, but the point is that humility can be a virtue even in competition. Humility is the fastest firefighter being able to compete in healthy competition while putting ability in perspective.

James Autry wrote that great leaders do not seek out angles that will make them great; rather, a leader's humility allows for effective leadership.[4] What this means is that a leader's *being* produces effective leadership, not tricks and tools. Moreover, a leader who is authentic and humble will inspire others. An authentic leader functions through relationships built upon trust.[5]

Researchers Bradley P. Owens and David R. Hekman studied the behaviors and outcomes of humble leaders and discovered that humility in leadership influences four areas.[6] The first is organization development and change. The humble leader is committed to the organization and the individual, and this commitment fosters positive change for both. Put another way, the humble leader understands that the organization *is* the individual, and collectively, the individuals are the organization. This relates to Spears' comment that servant-leaders have a commitment to the growth of their followers. It is an important point for those who wish to develop today's fire and emergency services professionals into tomorrow's leaders, because people who have been supported and groomed will be ready to lead the organization.[7] The humble leader understands that a leader who grows individuals also grows and develops the organization.

The second emergent factor Owens and Heckman discovered was that humility improved the relationship between leaders and followers. The humble leader within the fire and emergency services is approachable, not the stereotypical aloof, macho-gruff individual who has been written about by thoughtful observers.[8] Humble leaders keeps personal strengths, talents, and position in perspective, realizing that not everybody is like them or feels as they do.[9] Consistent humility promotes strong leader-follower relationships built on trust.

The third issue uncovered by Owens and Heckman's research was the relationship between a leader's humility and the engagement of followers. A humble leader fosters "ownership" of one's position. Fire Chief Rick Lasky wrote a book about the power of passion and ownership of one's position in the fire and emergency services, in which he noted that the more pride responders have in their positions, the more they own the position, make it personal, elevate it beyond just being a job.[10] Personal ownership fosters a dedication to one's people and profession. The humble leaders understand this; they engage their followers and foster pride. The followers in turn take ownership of their roles and responsibilities and contribute to the overall organization.

Owens and Heckman found that the fourth emergent aspect involved change to an organization's structural approach. A humble leader desires to hear from those at the bottom, the individuals most affected by decisions and policies. The people on the ground can give guidance on how to best deliver fire and emergency services to the public because they are the ones responding; they are the end-user of decisions.

In an interesting study, author and researcher Dr. Julie Exline found that humility was important for both the givers and receivers of acts of kindness, and reported on the literature that showed how humility leads to increased motivation and better performance in academics and on the job.[11] Other studies show that the humble leader is one whose leadership approach leads to healing and forgiveness Perhaps Larry Spears put it best: Healing involves both the healing of self as well as the healing of others.[12]

The humble leader desires to put others' worlds back together. Humility allows humanity to flourish; it is a commitment to forgive others as well as self for resulting decisions and practices. Humble leaders understand that if they cannot forgive, they cannot be forgiven, and without forgiveness, there is no healing; wounds will remain open. The healing of the individual, whether oneself or another, is imperative to success. A person cannot successfully function in a constant state of sadness. Self-blame and guilt that humans assume stifles progress; the servant-leader strives to heal these wounds for the good of the individual.

Dr. Exline showed how humility allows one to receive gratefully, the gifts, "thank-yous", or forgiveness from others.[13] Humility does not coexist comfortably with grudges. One must strive to seek forgiveness as well as forgive because grudges are destructive; they take up space in the soul. Furthermore, one's humility fosters personal generosity as well as a desire to help others. Even Robert Greenleaf discussed the notion of humility in leadership as a leader's ability to accept generously.[14] Here is a scenario to ponder:

> Imagine you are a lieutenant of a ladder company in a very poor fire district. Last week during a snowstorm, your company responded to an officer-assist call where an older woman had locked herself out of her apartment; the woman lived on the fourth floor. A police officer on patrol found her shivering in front of her building. The property owner could not be reached nor were any locksmiths available to respond due to the weather; regardless, the woman could never afford a locksmith. You decided to have your company deploy the aerial

ladder, climb up to and open a window of her apartment, and enter the structure from the outside of the building to unlock the door. In all, the operation took 10 minutes.

Later that week, the woman arrived at the fire station asking to see you. She had baked you and your crew a dessert and wanted to thank you for your work. Humbly, with an open heart you accepted this kind gesture. The operation your crew performed was mundane and somewhat trivial, but from that woman's perspective, you saved her—your crew put her world back together. Regardless of how trivial the operation, to her your actions were heroic. Understanding this, you did not play down the operation and you gratefully accepted her generosity.

Author and researcher Dr. Neal Krause found that humility was correlated with better health.[15] Fire and emergency services professionals need all the help they can get to stay healthy. The profession takes a heavy toll on responders, both physically and mentally.[16] Responder play witness to human tragedy. Upon arrival, they become a part of the situation; they are not bystanders. Humility allows a responder to gratefully receive the help and assistance that are so needed for his or her overall physical and mental health. Humility acknowledges that being invincible is a myth, that regardless of experience or training, humanity is fragile.

For the fire and emergency services leader, humility does not weaken but rather *strengthens* one's role, not only as a leader, but also as a team member.[17] Scholar and author Annette Suzanne Peters and her research colleagues discovered that arrogance, the antithesis of humility, had a negative effect on interpersonal relationships.[18] In the fire and emergency services, responders act as part of a team and humility seems to strengthen the team.

The humble leader is the honest leader.[19] The humble leader can speak truth to followers as well as truth to power. The humble leader makes the fair decision in all situations and does not hide behind policy to avert consequence.[20] To understand this point, we need to revisit the scenario from Chapter 1 involving the distraught firefighter asking for the night off.

> The firefighter came to your office after returning from an emergency medical services call where a vehicle struck a teenager in a crosswalk. The firefighter, a father of a disabled child, asked for the night off. On this call, he had been the patient technician providing advanced emergency medical care to the victim. During patient transport, the patient went into cardiac arrest and died. Instead of answering his request for a night off with "We just don't have the staffing and downtown is giving too much grief about using overtime," you asked if he was all right or needed to talk, then you granted him the night off and offered to set up a critical incident stress debriefing. You then called in an overtime to staff the firefighter's position.

In this revised scenario, even though you were protected by department policy to rule bureaucratically, your humility allowed you to make a fair and caring decision.[21] As a leader who loves your people, you defended your decision to your superiors and protected your firefighter. As a manager, you were in your right to say that staffing is an issue and deny the request for the night off. However, because you are a humble leader, you instead chose the compassionate thing to do.[22]

Research abundantly supports the efficacy of humility in a leader. Researchers Chan, McBey, and Scott-Ladd argued that humility was a virtue of the ethical leader.[23] Researchers Nielson, Marrone, and Slay found that followers were more committed to a humble leader's vision because the leader demonstrated empathy for their situations.[24] Again, this concept is not about being weak but real and trustworthy.[25] Researchers Grahek, Thompson, and Toliver found that the act of being humble is a testament to one's character and goes to the heart of a person being worthy to hold a position of leadership.[26]

Fire and emergency services leaders need to be empathetic to those they serve, and empathy relates directly to humility. Humility in fire and emergency services leaders drives their ability to be empathetic with their followers, as well as to those to whom they render aid. This is not always easy on the scene of an emergency response. It requires a balance of empathy for the situation of others while avoiding irrational or unwarranted judgment. Emergencies sometimes occur in dilapidated dwellings and dangerous locations and they often present to the responder the realities of poverty and human suffering. Empathy allows responders to be aware of the dangers while simultaneously performing their jobs.[28]

Researcher Dr. Jennifer Foster studied nurses working with the World Health Organization and found that humility, and *cultural* humility specifically, is the essential component to delivering healthcare on a global scale.[29] She learned that interaction over time between groups of people creates a natural humility, fostered by an understanding that can only stem from being together. Again, the notion is not that persons in leadership roles should become meek but, rather, to realize the innate dignity of humanity dictates that all people have worth.[30] The fire and emergency services responder cannot choose who receives care; the responder simply renders aid to all without question. Cultural humility involves an understanding of different healthcare needs and vulnerabilities relevant to different segments of a population.[31] Simply put, different people have different personal needs, as well as cultural needs and traditions that go along with who they are. In order to be successful, the fire and emergency services responder must understand these factors without judgment.

This is important because the fire and emergency services professionals form the frontline of the emergency healthcare system. Nationally, 85% to 95% of calls to fire and emergency services organizations are emergency medical responses.[32]

Like nurses, that makes fire and emergency services professionals essential to the healthcare system. The practice of cultural humility helps responders function in multiple situations involving diverse populations.

To refer to one's self as a fire and emergency services professional means that one must *act* professionally, which means going beyond the basic training and education needed to perform a task. Humility drives a desire to understand others, to appreciate the differences in cultures and people. Authors Robert Dennis and Mihai Bocarnea wrote that humility means, "viewing oneself as no better or worse than others do." [33] At its core, humility is about respect for others, empathy for the plight of the human condition, and the ability to be humane.

Other researchers have chimed in on the power of humility. Hayes and Comer argued that humility is humanity, and for the fire and emergency services, that a humble attitude is expressed outwardly with humanitarian acts of self-sacrifice and care. [34] The fire and emergency services responder deals with others in their most vulnerable situations in their most critical time of need.[35] Humility allows them to reach out to others in crisis situations.[36] An emergency medical technician's humility allows her to hold the hand of a dying man, knowing the act comforts him even though he cannot be saved. This is humanity in action.

Fire and emergency services professionals humbly engage in the lives of others. They render aid in others' times of need, and their leaders cannot lose sight of this. Everyone—leaders and followers—must foster their humility in order to maintain their humanity; this act is imperative to the overall well-being of the leader and follower. Only through humility can one accept personal limitations and not just render help, but also ask for it.[37]

CHAPTER 7

ALTRUISM

"And in the development of mankind as a whole, just as in individuals, love alone acts as a civilizing factor in the sense that it brings a change from egoism to altruism."

– Sigmund Freud

LEADERSHIP PRACTICED WITH ALTRUISM MEANS GIVING ONESELF to followers based upon the belief that acting for the betterment of others is a noble practice.[1] Altruism is an outward showing of one's humanity toward others and the practice of being altruistic is an expression of compassion and love.[2] Altruism does not diminish a leader but shifts the emphasis of giving to those being led. It is in no way a relinquishment of position.[3] For a fire and emergency services professional, altruism includes benevolence, the desire to do good unto others.

In its extreme expression, altruism in the fire and emergency services can mean sacrificing one's life for another. However, as one author noted, being an altruistic leader within a day-to-day setting means that self-interest need not be the only thing that matters; a love for self and a love for others can coexist.[4] There is a place for a grounded altruistic leader who gives unselfishly to others.

This chapter looks at two issues: altruistic leadership for the betterment of one's followers, and the altruistic behaviors that responders outwardly show to those they serve.

Fire and emergency services responders are public servants; their role is to serve others in their time of need and render aid or care. Responders exist solely for the public good and not personal gain, which means that the notion of altruism within the profession comes naturally and decisions should be made in the interest of those being served.[5]

Altruism stems from a core belief that if one is committed to others then the organization as a whole thrives.[6] An altruistic leader has a passion and desire to serve others.[7] An altruistic leader fosters community, possessing the ability to bring others together and empower them.[8]

We have learned from Larry Spears that building community is a general characteristic of servant-leaders, but community is especially important within the fire and emergency services because of the family-like conditions in which responders live.[9] Their shift schedules and close working conditions foster an *esprit de corps,* and without that, the work suffers.

A wise fire and emergency services leader builds, mentors, and coaches the crews because he or she realizes that only a cohesive team operating together can effectively deliver emergency services. These crews are made up of individuals with different needs. Health issues, leave, training, and equipment are just a few of the ongoing needs of team members; however, there are other needs as well, such as healing and the need to feel safe. The altruistic leader meets these needs, not by sacrificing self, but by giving one's self fully to those being led. That's altruism in action.

Researchers have found that a direct correlation exists between a strong showing of altruism from a leader and a positive environment, as well as successful outcomes.[10] What's more, individuals are able to perceive whether a leader truly cares and willingly gives of oneself to others.[11] Altruism shows as genuine happiness from the leader that springs from an inner joy, creating a natural, outward expression of love that is simply unmistakable and unavoidable.[12] Altruistic love begins with the core of the leader and spreads outwardly.[13]

You can't fake it. Followers know whether a leader is authentic; over a short period, unauthentic leaders realize it.[14] A leader's credibility is ruined when he or she attempts to be authentic in public and unauthentic in private.[15] Consider this:

> A fire department's battalion chief brags how his loyalty lies with his crew. He constantly jokes around with subordinates and tells stories to his superiors of how he defends the "fellas". In a public attempt to be perceived as a listener, the battalion chief solicits followers' opinions on issues, but rarely utilizes the information. His actions speak far more than his words. The battalion chief is actually a sycophant; his true intent is promotion. Fortunately, his followers realize this. As hard as he tries to be an authentic leader; he never will be one because his credibility will always remain in question. He is not altruistic to his followers; he is irrationally self-serving, and his team knows it.

The unique demands of the profession make altruism a virtue. Unlike many work situations where leader decisions are based on non-life-threatening situations, the fire and emergency services leader is responsible not only for the situation, but also to team members long before and long after the emergency. Altruism in this setting has a practical side. It means that you take the extra time to ensure that responders receive proper training. If there has been a bad call, discuss it with them, and if necessary, follow up. An altruistic leader in the fire and emergency services is not one who sacrifices self for others, but one who gives of oneself to others out of benevolence.[16]

To argue for altruistic leadership within the fire and emergency services is not a stretch; the profession practically demands it. After all, fire and emergency services professionals are public servants. Citizens do not question the responders' role of service and *expect* them to render the care and aid to strangers with the same compassion and concern they would to a close friend or loved one. This is altruism, the giving of oneself without reciprocity. One can argue that the reciprocity is financial compensation; however, in the case of many responders, especially those who volunteer, compensation can be paltry and even non-existent, depending on their position or organization.

The second main point of this chapter is that altruism already exists within the fire and emergency services, so altruistic leadership should naturally emerge from an altruistic profession.

Fire and emergency services professionals respond to diverse communities of cultures, languages, religious beliefs, lifestyles, and demographics. Though diversity is in no way a negative, it poses a challenge to responders, as they are called upon to answer all emergencies, having no idea what the next encounter will reveal regarding language, religion, or domestic encounters. Responders approach these challenges altruistically. They do not respond using a diversity matrix or decide how much aid and care to render based upon different demographics. Instead, they respond as ethical public service leaders, free of irrational judgment and bigotry, willing to give of themselves for others through their jobs.

Research conducted around the world shows that ethical leadership spans cultures.[17] It fosters relationships and builds trust; and, since trusted, congruent, ethical leadership leads to positive outcomes across cultures, the altruistic leader stands a better chance of operating among diverse populations.[18] That is the primary reason fire and emergency professionals are widely trusted: they respond out of altruism, giving themselves to the community they serve.

The system works because an altruistic leader functions better than a non-altruistic leader when dealing with social issues.[19] This construct of trust makes it easier to build a community of understanding within a diverse society, and it starts with creating policies and laws that govern emergency and disaster responses.[20] Author Russell Dynes referred to this as situational altruism, a behavior that strives to find out what actually works during disasters and why, , regardless of community.[21]

Altruism also leads to better emergency and disaster *planning* to support communities in times of need.[22] Studies reveal that ordinary citizens also want to help in times of crisis, even if only to forget awhile that they are also victims.[23] This widespread altruistic impulse, especially during large-scale emergencies, is something that can be used in planning for disasters, and it reveals the common humanity that exists between people.[24]

Mention a firefighter, emergency medical technician, or emergency worker and most citizens conjure up images of heroes. Photographs, book covers, and films frequently depict the heroic responder as an individual, perhaps with a face smeared with soot, carrying a helpless child in to safety.[25] People in emergencies focus on the flesh-and-blood responder who always shows up when called upon and saves the day, against all odds. In the public's mind, responders are *expected* to be altruistic, and with good reason, because altruism lives within the soul of the responder. To argue for an altruistic approach to leadership within fire and emergency services is to simply affirm what is already true about this population of remarkable professionals.

For examples, one needs to look no further than annual line-of-duty death reports published by the National Fire

Academy. In a twenty-year span, close to 500 fire and emergency services responders were killed in the line of duty while performing just search and rescue operations.[26] One such incident involved a firefighter who gave his life to save his leader, a fire lieutenant; unfortunately, both the leader and follower perished [27]:

> In 2009, the Buffalo Fire Department in New York responded to a structure fire at a convenience store. During the operation, Lieutenant Charles McCarthy, Jr. fell into the basement of the building when the first floor collapsed. At the time of the collapse, Lieutenant McCarthy was tasked with ensuring that all firefighting personnel had exited the structure due to worsening interior conditions.[28] Firefighter Jonathan Croom, after hearing mayday calls from Lieutenant McCarthy, immediately entered the structure to search for him. During the search and rescue operations, both Lieutenant McCarthy's and Firefighter Croom's SCBAs ran out of air. During recovery efforts, the men were found near each other in the basement.[29] Both Lieutenant McCarthy and Firefighter Croom died in service to others while engaging in acts of altruistic sacrifice.

When they are invited into the lives of others, fire and emergency services responders become humble servants who, when called upon, are willing to give their all.[30] The sacrifice illustrated in the deaths of Lieutenant McCarthy and Firefighter Croom is the purest form of Patterson's definition of altruism: giving of oneself for another. Altruism flows from a core passion to serve others without question or hesitation, and a willingness to give one's own life in the process.[31]

People who are willing to sacrifice their lives for others deserve leaders who are willing to sacrifice themselves to them. This is not asking too much from fire and emergency services leaders, for they were once such followers, and the altruistic impulse remains.[32]

CHAPTER 8

VISION

"Throughout the centuries there were men who took first steps, down new roads, armed with nothing but their own vision."

– Ayn Rand

THIS CHAPTER LOOKS AT PATTERSON'S CONSTRUCT OF *VISION* and the place it has within fire and emergency services leadership—specifically as it pertains to organizational, community, and follower needs.

Patterson found that Greenleaf explicitly argued that a servant-leader needs to have a commitment to vision, the ability to personally understand a desired future and communicate it to others. When leaders and managers asked Greenleaf's advice about organizational situations, he frequently answered with questions that required them to articulate their vision, such as: "Who do you want to be?" and "What do you want to do?"[1] Sadly, many could not answer these questions, especially the first one.

Patterson also stated that the construct of vision included a leader's ability to both recognize and foster the strengths of others. Vision ensures that an individual's gifts, talents, and abilities are not squandered but are honed and supported. This is not simply an issue of personnel development, but also one of *morality*.[2] To ignore a person's strengths and abilities is immoral. The visionary leader continuously cultivates a person's unique abilities and realizes where to use those abilities to benefit the organization.

Vision relies upon a servant-leader's ability to practice *foresight*, which means understanding present trends so deeply that one can access intuition and see just over the horizon.[3] In fact, Greenleaf said that foresight is the only "lead" a leader has and it informs a servant-leader's evolution of vision.[4] Vision, in turn, guides a servant-leader's commitment to the growth of others, which is necessary to address future needs.[5] You can pretty much judge a servant-leader's vision by looking at whether followers are ready to operate successfully in the future.

Finally, both Patterson and Greenleaf argued that vision was closely related to conceptualization, the ability to "zoom out" and see the big picture, to think holistically. If you cannot see the future needs of those you serve nor conceptualize the processes and programs to meet said needs, you cannot successfully lead.[6] A leader with an inability to foresee and conceptualize the future is simply a place keeper, and followers and those being served will suffer.

A majority of leadership texts discuss the subject of vision. Researchers Vinod and Sudhakar argued that the core role of a leader is setting a vision that defines the direction of an organization.[7] Vision evokes the future; you could even say that the overall success of a leader *depends* upon the ability to envision and communicate a possible future.[8] These days, organizations cannot simply exist in the present and stand a chance in the future. They need visionary leaders for survival.[9] Civilization has evolved following the roadmaps of visionaries, people who try to understand past and present at a deep level in order to sense the needs and trends of the future. This is called the art of knowing the next step.[10]

Some people argue that fire and emergency services organizations exist solely for emergency response, that their role remains the same while the needs of society change and the organization can simply address and adapt to presenting situations. The fact is, a leader in any organization who discounts vision must be prepared to accept great challenges. The same holds true for leaders in the fire and emergency services. It is imperative for them to see the needs of all whom they serve and deliver that vision successfully.[11]

Greenleaf believed that a leader who lacked foresight—an ability to vision the future—failed an *ethical* duty of leadership because people can be needlessly hurt when their leaders blindly stumble into disasters that could have been avoided.

Researcher J. Thomas Whetstone also referred to vision as part of moral leadership, the notion that the leader must be committed to the betterment of the institution and an ongoing state of thriving, not just surviving.[12] This leader defends the organization's future by holding firm to a commitment to its people, understanding that they make up the organization; therefore, an organization and its people are one in the same.[13] Adverse consequences are associated with failing to have or adhere to a vision, and the moral leader is completely aware of these consequences.[14] Anyone who has worked in fire and emergency services operations for only a few years could offer stories that illustrate the pain derived from a lack of foresight, and history is riddled with tales about preventable fires and emergencies that cause loss of property, injury, and even death. People who study such things say that most fires of the past that decimated great cities could have been avoided.[15] Tragically, the same holds true today.

When vision, foresight, and conceptualization lack within the fire and emergency services, the picture is bleak. People can suffer from poor planning regarding disasters, urban planning, and resource needs. A lack of vision and foresight exacerbate problems associated with aging construction, timely responses to urban sprawl, population growth, urban wild-land interfacing, changing demographics, methods of people-moving, and politically related pressures.

To make matters more complicated, bureaucratic push-back and political pressures may compromise even leaders with vision and foresight. Faced with the ignorant attitude of "*It has never happened before, so why do we need to do it now?*" fire and emergency services leaders find themselves in constant battles they often lose. When tragedy occurs, however, those same leaders are held responsible and receive the majority of the blame.

The duties of fire and emergency services professionals have changed over time.[16] The once simple yet important role of responding only to fires is now a complex system that requires professionals to deliver skills and take responsibility for all-hazards fire and emergency services responses. Along the way, some leaders envisioned and implemented changes, but too often, unplanned-for tragedies and outside entities forced changes not based upon vision and not implemented with substantial discussion or buy-in from on-ground teams. Sadly, many organizations ignored, or worse, pushed back against visionary changes, such as fire and emergency services preparing for an all-hazards approach to service. For example, in many organizations, fire and emergency service leaders had to fight to convince members to accept emergency medical services as part of their responsibility. Today, 85% to 95% of the calls to most fire and emergency services organizations involve emergency medical responses. Many fire and emergency services organizations cannot justify their existence without advanced life support emergency medical services.

I repeat that successful leaders must have a vision and the ability to lead the vision by serving those who will carry it out.[17] Landing on the moon is a prime example. In the 1960s, the United States of America did not have a race to just *any-where*, nor did it strive to land on just *anything*. Instead, the country responded to President Kennedy's *specific* challenge to end the decade by landing a man on the moon and returning him safely to earth. By 1969 the mission was accomplished by engineers, scientists, administrators, subcontractors, and astronauts. The president did not do it alone. He defined the possible reality of the vision and turned loose his experts, and the entire world continues to benefit.

Successful CEO and author Max De Pree made a stunning statement about leadership: "The first responsibility of a leader is to define reality. The last is to say thank you. In between the two, the leader must become a servant and a debtor."[18] As evidenced by the space race, a leader who offers a vision inspires others' to follow.[19] Just any vision won't do; it must be inspiring and point to an ongoing evolution of positive change and growth. A vision that is shared between leaders and followers leads to success.[20] Now here is the scary part for control freaks: implementing the shared vision requires *decentralized* decision-making.[21] That does not mean there is no accountability; we are talking about accountability *without* micromanaged control. Consider again the space race. Leaders and followers shared the vision; leaders led and followers carried it out, each making local decisions that led to the overall success of the space program, and each was accountable for those decisions.

Because of the fear of losing power and control, some leaders reject decentralized decision-making. This is not the case for a servant-leader, however. Decentralized decision-making under the umbrella of a shared vision comes easily to servant-leaders because they understand their power is based upon their ability to persuade people and trust them to make prudent decisions. The *real* power of servant-leaders comes to them as a gift from their followers.[22] Servant-leaders also understand that followers can withdraw their freely-given power if the leaders breech the followers' sacred trust by acting in coercive or autocratic ways.

In the confusion of an emergency scene, decentralized decision-making is a *necessity*. The leader with the positional authority—that is, the official title—cannot see or respond to every development. Acting under a shared vision and using a model of decentralized decision-making, the followers—professionals with boots on the ground and rescue ladders in the sky—can carry out the shared vision beyond direct control by seeing the situation and its needs from their close perspective, making needed choices, and having those decisions supported by their superiors.[23]

People who have never worked in the fire and emergency services may not understand the complicated split-second decisions that must be made in chaotic situations. How do you attack this fire? Where do you place your resources? Does the team have enough resources at hand? What are the changing safety concerns? How will injured victims be cared for and transported? These speed-of-light choices occur in real time and under pressure.

Leaders and team professionals make flash decisions based upon what they see working in the moment, upon both positive and negative past experiences, training, and education. They know their superiors gifted them the power to make choices on the spot, to be a *leader* where the action is.

It may be difficult for a layman to understand the sweep of activities in this profession. Response apparatus may be staged over vast geographical areas, and each organization responds to multiple calls. Fire and emergency services professionals operate day-to-day in small teams, ranging from two partners on an ambulance to crews of three to five personnel staffing engines, aerials, and special rescue companies.

These companies respond solo to alarms and emergency service calls.[24]

At an emergency, the senior officer on-scene is the incident commander. Upon arrival, the on-scene commander puts a plan of attack into action.[25] Often times, the individual making the on-scene decision is unaware of why the plan formed the way it did in his or her mind. An on-scene commander's plan of attack develops from prior experiences, prior training and education, department policies and procedures, and the conditions upon arrival. These issues come together to form a decision, and the decision then becomes the order relayed to on-scene and responding crews. The decision made and the order given, based upon the aforementioned issues, forms the leader's vision of what it will take to be successful. In this case, the leader, in a very short period, uses historical knowledge coupled with present conditions to envision the future; specifically, the mitigation of the problem.

Now you begin to see why, in this profession, organizations *must* decentralize leadership and empower company level officers, and at times, senior, non-officer fire and emergency service responders, to make decisions. In few work situations is it this clear that success depends upon followers being empowered to carry out the organization's vision.[26]

This is a practical way of operating on-scene. Fire and emergency services professionals often operate in pairs or small response teams without chief-officer supervision present, especially executive officer supervision. Two paramedics in an ambulance or a single engine company may be the only ones responding to an incident. Such responses can involve something as simple as resetting a fire alarm or deciding what level to use in transporting a patient to the hospital. Responses can also involve far more complex issues for fire and emergency services companies, such as developing new response matrixes, criteria for their district, or establishing and carrying out on-scene command and control of a major incident until more resources arrive. Regardless of the type or size of the task, it is all done on a solid foundation of shared vision and take-action empowerment, without checking every detail with the chief or commander, who may not be on-scene. Choices are also made in the clear knowledge that everyone—leaders and followers—will be held accountable for their decisions.

Let's summarize: The fire and emergency services leader has the responsibility to lead effectively.[27] Research has found that there is a relationship between a leader's effectiveness and a leader's vision.[28] The fire and emergency services leader has the responsibility of fostering positive leader-follower relationships within the organization and providing effective leadership to the community being served. This responsibility exists both on and off scene in the planning phases of an emergency and in the future needs of a community, from population growth to infrastructure changes. So vision must be at the center of their responsibility to their own teams, *and* to the community. They must understand why vision is so important and clarify it to all audiences.[29]

A vision is clarified through words *and* actions to make it a reality—seeing to effective training and education, disseminating information in an accurate and timely manner, ensuring that follower's mental and physical health needs are met and that their questions are being answered.[30] For the community, visionary leadership means meeting and understanding community needs in order to strengthen resiliency in future emergencies.[31] It means walking the streets, talking to people, and reading the latest research about the community's demographic makeup in order to effectively envision future needs.[32] Finally, a visionary leader shares with professional team members and the broader community the substance of the vision and the reasons why it is important. The act of sharing the vision will elicit suggestions that could improve it.

As obvious as it may seem, many old-school leaders seem to forget that the reason for sharing the vision with team members is because *they are the ones who will be carrying it out.*[33] A leader who does not clarify the vision, can assume it is *not* understood. Even when an organization practices shared vision, the leader remains ultimately responsible for initially establishing and accomplishing it.[34]

Research has shown that an organization that has a leader with vision receives high levels of performance from followers.[35] Moreover, there is a relationship between vision and the empowerment of followers; essentially the visionary leader brings individuals together in shared responsibility and commitment to the vision.[36] Thus, the visionary leader is a builder of community within an organization, a community whose foundation consists of a mutual commitment to the vision.[37]

The visionary rejects complacency and looks toward the future.[38] Inwardly, vision protects the fire and emergency services profession, keeping the career field viable by meeting future needs. [39] The fire and emergency services professional remains committed to being at the ready by taking on different responsibilities for both the individuals within the organization as well as the community in which they serve.[40] In order to be successful, it all comes down to the leader's ability to vision a future and meet the needs of all they serve.

CHAPTER 9

TRUST

"If a man's associates find him guilty of being phony, if they find that he lacks forthright integrity, he will fail. His teachings and actions must square with each other. The first great need, therefore, is integrity and high purpose."

– *President Dwight D. Eisenhower*

TRUST IS CENTRAL TO SUCCESSFUL RELATIONSHIPS BETWEEN individuals, groups, and organizations.[1] Trust is based on the belief that the other party will act truthfully. For the fire and emergency services, trust is essential to effective emergency operations.[2] It binds and sustains relationships.[3]

When Patterson identified trust as a construct of servant leadership, she was influenced by the research of Melani Fletcher, who found that trust is the foundation of leadership.[4] Patterson also reflected on the idea of integrity, a characteristic that seemingly encompassed the other constructs of servant leadership, and realized that *trust* is what allows others to have faith in a leader's integrity.

As with power, trust is a gift that can be taken away, and once it is gone it is difficult to regain. Leaders have a duty to recognize that the organization's future becomes jeopardized when they lose the trust of followers, and followers need to understand that when leaders question their trustworthiness due to actions, inactions, or events, regaining trust is difficult and at times impossible. Imagine:

> You are a captain in charge of two stations in an outlying area. A battalion chief just finished scolding you about one of your officers, a young lieutenant in charge of a rescue company. It seems this new lieutenant is striving hard for acceptance by his rescue crew; he wants to be seen as cool and liked. The crew, as noted in the scolding from the battalion chief, seems to be taking liberties far beyond department policy. Several members of the crew have had more days off than calculated and reported as leave on their timecards. This has been going on for several pay-periods; and, by chance, the department's human resources officer just noticed the discrepancy when looking at personnel detailed to that crew. The timecards have the crewmembers' initials next to the leave they were charged, as well as the lieutenant's signature. You as the captain do not see these timecards; they are submitted directly to the system. You do have access to them, yet have chosen to trust your junior officers.
>
> As the lieutenant's superior officer, you are ultimately responsible for this. You trusted the lieutenant, as you did any of your other officers. This, however, is a breach of trust and you confront the lieutenant, who admits his wrongdoings. You decide to double-check every piece of paper with this man's signature in the near future. You also decide to detail him to another crew and remove some of his authority. The lieutenant has lost your trust and put your position in jeopardy, as you yourself faced possible demotion and termination due to timecard fraud under your command. Ask yourself, how long would it take you to trust this lieutenant again? What about other junior officers—do you now question them, too, due to the actions of one?

Lost trust creates a myriad of interpersonal issues, not only between the two people involved—in this example, two officers—but also between your timecard cheater and every person he or she deals with in the future. Regaining trust is difficult.[5] It takes time and repeated proofs that a person is once again trustworthy. Rebuilding trust is an enormous, yet essential, task for future successes and organizational survival.[6] If you were the captain in the example just cited, trusting others beyond doing their jobs—that is, trusting their character, honesty, and congruent actions—would be a testament to your strength.

Here is what some key research articles say about trust: Trust creates an environment where all parties have faith in one another to always do the right thing and never betray that principle.[7] Trust directly relates to ethical behavior—doing what is right and always being honest and forthcoming.[8] Trust equates to moral duty.[9] Trust supports both leaders and followers, for if leaders are trusted, then others seek to follow.[10] The leader-follower relationship is simpler when leading and following exist naturally in an atmosphere of trust. It really is that simple. When people trust their leaders, they desire to follow them, and in the process gift power to the leader.[11]

There is more. You will find that within the fire and emergency services, responders strive for assignments with trusted company and battalion level leaders. The do not need to read the research to know that following a trusted leader directly relates to job satisfaction and that they are more likely to be happier and feel more fulfilled.[12]

Because this profession operates within team structures, the teams are only as good as their relationships and cohesiveness.[13] Fire and emergency services leaders must understand that team cohesiveness begins with developing familiarity between members; it is through this familiarity that trust develops.[14] Negativity and lack of job satisfaction plays havoc with a team's structure. Thus, a satisfied team that is built upon trust and respect thrives.

Successful fire and emergency services teams begin with trust because the profession operates in situations where each individual responder has responsibility.[15] Trust is a critical factor to building strong team effectiveness.[16]

If you look at an engine company with four individuals, you will find three sets of responsibilities. (1) The officer in charge of the company has the overall responsibility of the crew, including decision-making. (2) The engineer is responsible for safely operating the apparatus, ensuring that all tools, equipment, and fluids are present. In addition, the engineer needs to know the route and vehicle placement. (3) The firefighters have the responsibility of carrying out the officer's orders, selecting and using the proper equipment, and knowing their role on the emergency scene.

Each of these individuals joins the others to form a team. Collectively, they trust that each member knows his or her job and will do what is needed. As a team, each member trusts the others, as trust is a critical factor in building strong team effectiveness.[17] In fact, the nature of the profession demands it.[18] You have heard the cliché that a team is only as good as its weakest member. Because of the danger involved in fire and emergency services, you can also say that the *safety* of every member is only as good as the safety mindset of its weakest member, and team members literally trust each other with their lives.

Trust is not a given in this environment. Each member must prove himself or herself—literally, under fire. Team members need to have faith in one another to trust each other.[19] They must experience each one's abilities, in training and in the field.

The reality of trusting teams begins in the fire and emergency services academy where active members of the organization become instructors responsible for training and mentoring newly-hired recruits. The recruits are, in actuality, asking these instructors to be part of their team, to be one of them, because they want to begin building cohesiveness with instructors who will accept them into their own ranks upon graduation and probation. They are, in short, asking to be trusted. During academy training, as well as the probationary period, recruits strive to perform in ways that demonstrate their abilities. They are outwardly showing the regular members of the organization that they are worthy rookies and can be trusted.

Communication is an essential component of effective teams, especially fire and emergency services teams.[20] Communication strengthens trust in every setting, but especially within fire and emergency services teams.[21] Failures in communication are often cited in after-action reports. A breakdown in communications can make things go terribly wrong in an already bad incident. Each member of the team needs to know what is going on, what is expected, who is where, and who is doing what. Adherence to strong communication protocols—from checking for fresh batteries in handheld walkie-talkies to using the correct terminology to describe a situation and give orders—reduces freelancing, guesswork, and most of all, tragedy.

The exact opposite exists where trust is lacking. Without trust, organizations suffer, individuals falter, and failure becomes inevitable.[22] The leader must desire for others to trust him or her, and gain that trust through behavior and ethical practices. One cannot demand trust; it is earned as a gift from others.[23]

To re-emphasize, trust is critical to successful leadership. The best leaders understand that building trust takes hard work and sustaining trust is even harder.[24] But it is a beautiful thing to behold when it works. With trust, responders believe in the abilities of those in command positions to make the right decisions and they are willing to carry out orders without question.[25]

The emergency scene requires responders to rely on not only their own abilities, but also the abilities of others.[26] Fire and emergency services leaders must learn to delegate to their followers. The nature of selective emergency response squelches any impulses leaders may have to micromanage all aspects of an organization. Geographical area and multiple responses mean that companies operate independently. At best, department policy, protocols, and written procedures govern guidelines of independent operations, but no policy can foresee every possible situation. Studies have shown that delegation—even though uncomfortable for some leaders—actually *strengthens* followers' trust in their leaders.[27]

Another way of looking at trust within the fire and emergency services is that it drives a continuous cycle of interpretation and understanding.[28] The on-scene commander gives the order to place equipment on the right side of a burning building because he has information that a shipping department storing highly-combustible materials is located there. The firefighter, who has less information about the situation, nevertheless trusts his leader and asks his fellow firefighters to help. One firefighter who notices that the bulk of the fire seems to be on the left side of the building at the moment rather than the right side does his job anyway because he trusts the order. The commander, who is busy with multiple demands, finds time to come by and explain the threat on the right side. While he is there the firefighter in charge passes along information about a new safety threat—not everyone in the building is yet accounted for. This continuous cycle of trust not only makes for effective emergency responses but places the responsibility of sustaining trust not just on the leader, but also the follower.[29] This is the short version: *trust falls on the shoulders of everyone.*

This short example illustrates that trust is imperative when making decisions under emergency conditions, and how leaders and followers participate in collective sense-making within an emergency operation.[30] Collective sense-making means both leaders and followers trust each other to make the right decisions and pass along critical information. The leader can make the ultimate decision; however, it is up to the followers to develop the specific micro actions to carry out the decision. Another example:

> A chief officer arrives on-scene of a confirmed structure fire late at night. Upon arrival, a man approaches him stating that he rents a room on the second floor to a woman whose car is parked on the street and yet she is nowhere to be found. The man states that he and his wife heard the woman come home earlier in the evening. The chief officer gives the structure a 360-degree size-up and issues an order. Because this is a life-safety issue, he orders the first-due company on arrival to search the structure and locate the missing woman. The chief officer relays to the incoming crews that the woman resides in a second floor room of the structure. The first company to arrive is a truck company, and they immediately perform a search and rescue operation as ordered, locating the woman unconscious yet alive.

In this scenario, the collective sense-making begins with the on-scene commander making an evaluation, ordering an immediate search and rescue operation, and then the truck company carrying out the order. The truck company trusted the decisions of the chief officer, trusted that the conditions and the risk-versus-reward calculation were worth it, and trusted that the woman was most likely trapped in the structure. Next, the chief officer trusted the truck company to carry out a successful search and rescue operation, make wise decisions on how to conduct the search, and choose the proper tools and tactics to perform the operation.

In this scenario, the followers—in this case, the truck company—had faith in their chief, which allowed them to have trust in him.[31] That trust, in turn, gave them faith that the chief's decisions were the right ones.

Fire and emergency services leaders need to realize that how they act, how they present themselves to the team and the world, and the way they treat others either builds or sabotages their trustworthiness.[32] When a leader is perceived to be trustworthy, followers view them as ethical stewards of the organization.[33] When followers view a leader as ethical, they gift power to him or her. The leader is then free to make decisions and establish a vision for the organization based upon followers trusting him or her.

Trust is crucial to the success of an organization.[34] For the fire and emergency services, trust is essential for successful operations and ultimately mitigating the emergency. The power of trust goes beyond the emergency scene, however. Within the political process that exists in the fire and emergency services, trustworthiness is the key to successful negotiations and relationships.[35] It is also critical in maintaining support from the wider community itself. After all, elected officials govern the fire and emergency services, and these officials serve their constituents. It behooves the fire and emergency services to know for whom they work and to develop strong, trust-based relationships with them, relationships that stem from ethical behavior and honorable practices.

In truth, the wider community being served is the recipient of trust's existence or lack thereof. Since trust is a component of ethical behavior, ethical behavior practices are the essential components of building trust between the fire and emergency services and the public at large.[36]

To summarize: a leader earns trust in the fire and emergency services; it does not come automatically with a position.[37]

Instead, it comes over time through a leader's actions.[38] Furthermore, followers must earn the leader's trust through their actions, commitment, and abilities to get the job done without direct supervision.[39] Followers are more likely to trust leaders if they feel they are being supported by the leader.[40]

Trust among leaders, followers, and those being served is what makes the work of fire and emergency services responders effective and meaningful.[41] Trust drives effective teamwork.[42] In fact, a team cannot function successfully without trust.[43]

Servant leadership is about building trust, and that alone is a reason for arguing for the practice of servant leadership within the fire and emergency services. Empirically, there is a direct correlation between the practice of servant leadership and trust within an organization.[44] If you want to be a leader in this profession, you must understand that it is your responsibility to strive to build an entire organization of trust.[45]

Servant leadership makes sense in the fire and emergency services because no other leadership philosophy holds trust so dear as one of its constructs.

CHAPTER 10

EMPOWERMENT

"Servant-leadership is all about making the goals clear and then rolling your sleeves up and doing whatever it takes to help people win. In that situation, they don't work for you, you work for them."

– *Ken Blanchard*

PATTERSON'S SIXTH CONSTRUCT OF SERVANT LEADERSHIP IS empowerment, a practice foundational to the practice of servant leadership. Empowerment is the policy of trusting others with responsibility by gifting to them the ability to make decisions, and therefore developing them as leaders.[1] By devolving appropriate authority to individuals, a servant-leader is actively expressing a commitment to the growth of team members and, yes, even a willingness to risk that they may make a mistake along the way. Empowerment changes the relationship between leaders and followers by changing responsibilities.[2]

Let's look at some of the benefits of empowerment.

Studies show that empowerment does more than encourage individual growth; it also leads to organizational commitment and loyalty because it gives individuals a sense of ownership.[3] There is a positive correlation between the level of empowerment and organizational commitment— higher empowerment leads to greater commitment.[4] Deeper commitment, in turn, leads to richer, more meaningful pride in the organization.

Rick Lasky, who was a dynamic fire chief before becoming an author and consultant, has explored the importance of what he calls *pride and ownership* within the fire and emergency services. Lasky writes that ownership leads to pride in three areas: in the responders' roles, in the organization they serve, and in the profession. Ultimately, says Lasky, pride comes from *love*—love of the job and love of the people who do the job.[5]

The fire and emergency services is a stressful occupation that wears at the soul of the responder.[6] Stress can lead to poor health and job burnout, and responders need all the help they can get in relieving stress. Believe it or not, empowerment can help.[7] Because empowerment gives meaning and purpose beyond following orders, it also increases employee retention.[8] After all, why would you abandon a job you love, even a demanding one like a responder, when you are allowed to make decisions that make a difference? Moreover, recent research shows that attitudes of feeling powerless and unneeded seem to contribute to post-traumatic stress disorder.[9]

Studies aside, all of this makes perfect sense and rings true with common experience. When proven team members are not allowed to make decisions and share in the vision, they can easily become distant. That distance whittles away at responders' resilience to stressful situations and makes them more vulnerable to the lingering effects of dangerous experiences and trauma, especially during their overtime hours.

Empowerment is more than a commitment to share decision-making. It leads to a *shared identity* between leaders and followers, bonding everyone to a commitment to the organizational vision.[10] It encourages personal ownership, healthy pride in the profession, and commitment to those with whom one serves and those who are being served. It even promotes safety and wellbeing.

The benefits of empowerment are multiplied in volunteer organizations. In the United States, volunteer firefighters outnumber paid firefighters three to one. Empowerment energizes volunteers. They feel more useful, an important part of the enterprise. They also experience personal satisfaction and a commitment to the organization, and choose to stay involved rather than drift on to the next volunteer opportunity. They are willing to serve simply for the privilege of serving and need to feel appreciated for their efforts.[11]

Sharing the vision is part and parcel of empowerment, and is considered a best practice in the fire and emergency services.[12] What does "sharing the vision" mean? Typically, it means that one or more designated leaders crank out a vision statement for the department and then "share" it with everyone else. They then expect followers to "buy into" the vision. When you look at this typical scenario, you see that it is another expression of the top-down mindset. To be sure, some parts of a vision really *must* be embraced by all responders, like a commitment to safety, but just possibly *everyone* in the department has something to contribute to the vision, even the newest recruit just out of the Academy. At minimum, everyone who is affected by a vision should have a chance to reflect on what the vision statement says and what it means to them in their designated jobs.

That said, the vision should be shared, accepted, and owned by followers because *they* are the ones who move it from words on the page to actions on the scene. A vision is a collective enterprise. A centralized vision held by the leader alone is worthless, but one that is owned by all is a dynamic, living force that makes responders want to get up in the morning and go to work.

Here is a major irony about empowerment. The profession is *all about* empowerment. Officers do not clear everything they do with a central location; there is seldom enough time for that. By necessity, responders are empowered to make decisions on-scene. Yet there are those who dismiss the wisdom of empowering others, not realizing that they themselves are being empowered. Which is to say that fire and emergency services leaders experience pushback about empowerment from within their own ranks.[13] Those who question the notion seem to mistakenly understand empowerment as a *laissez-faire* practice.[14] These naysayers argue that empowerment means a lack of rank structure or freelancing. The truth is, empowerment has nothing to do with any of these misconceptions.

Like any other organization, fire and emergency services adopt policies and procedures as well as standing orders and guidelines. Having these rules in place *makes empowerment possible*. The rules exist so leaders and followers clearly understand their boundaries. Guidelines are used as the approved context for making decisions, but leaders still make their own decisions. The very existence of these operating guidelines dispels the myth that empowerment within the fire and emergency services goes against the existing rank structure, or creates a *laissez-faire* approach towards leadership. They prove that the practice of empowering followers is not *carte blanche*: followers cannot pick and choose how and where they will accept empowerment and leaders cannot empower a rookie who has not yet learned the job to make strategic decisions.

Perhaps some (but not all) of those who resist empowerment have a deeper reason for their hesitancy: they sense that empowerment will change the flow of organizational operations and introduce unknown shifts of power. Or, they may simply be wary of change. We are all subject to the fear of change and hesitant to change for change's sake, so it's understandable when resisters need to be reassured that a different way of doing things will be better. What they need is *trust* in the process.

Trust is at the heart of empowerment, as it is in so many dynamics of servant leadership. From a leader-follower perspective, the construct of trust stems from having faith in others, thus leading to willingness to empower.[15] So lack of trust, rather than wariness of the process, is also a major factor that creates resistance to empowerment.

No one denies that followers must earn the faith and trust of their leaders before their leaders gift them the responsibility of empowerment. A prudent leader is one who only empowers followers after careful observation of their attitudes and abilities and engages in calculated, rational reflection. There is nothing *laissez-faire* about it.[16] A leader who understands this, and who has trained responders to understand the adopted rules and guides, can overcome the fears associated with empowerment.

The trust issue goes both ways. Followers need to feel safe with *being* empowered, which means they must also trust their leaders, not only for their knowledge and sincerity but also for their willingness to stand by them when decisions may be called into question.[17] It's called *The leader has your back!* On a daily basis, chief and company level officers, paramedics, and senior responders are called upon to make decisions involving life and death scenarios. With that kind of pressure, they *need* to believe that their leaders support them. Absent neglect or malice, responders cannot live in fear of making a bad decision. This creates undue stress and can actually lead to a wrong decision based on second-guessing what the chief might say.[18]

To further illustrate the need for trust and empowerment, one needs to look no further than the organizational structure of fire and emergency services organizations. The typical fire and emergency services response organization consists of multiple, independent companies controlled by junior officers who operate in designated strategic areas.[19] Companies and crews are empowered to respond to emergencies and make tactical and medical decisions free from the direct supervision of chief officers, depending on the size and severity of the situation.[20] In essence, the fire and emergency services profession operates in a *continuous* state of trust and empowerment. There is no other way to look at it. Leaders empower their officers to lead and officers empower their people to do their job.

The difficulty for executive level fire and emergency services leaders with titles like chief or deputy chief is their detachment from the daily operations and needs of their people. This is especially true in organizations with several hundred or even thousands of personnel spread over a vast geographical area.[21] The roles and responsibilities associated with personnel and daily operations are often delegated to subordinate battalion level chief officers. Reporting to them are the company level officers, often known as captains. Each captain often has several lieutenants reporting to him or her, as well as his or her own crew. When one looks at this vast network, it is easy to see how the structure creates a canyon between the overall chief executive and front line responders.

This wide chasm leaves a chief in a bubble, meaning the chief only hears from his or her executive level officers and these officers are hearing from battalion level chief officers who report to them and so on down the line. There is no rational explanation to justify centralized control over such a vast organizational structure when it is impossible to be everywhere at once. The executive level chief officers, even if they desire to micromanage, cannot be omnipresent at spread out companies, especially when simultaneous emergencies occur.

A thoughtful fire and emergency services executive should come to terms with this complex reality and realize that followers need to be empowered throughout the organizational structure. This, of course, requires a balance between positional authority and the reality of fire and emergency services operations.[22] Wise executives have learned the trick of building an alternate system based on *accountability without micro-control.*

A leader who chooses to empower others as a matter of policy is moving away from the centralized leadership tendencies adhered to by so many in power.[23] This brings new people into the mix, with all their collective wisdom and energy. Here is another irony: by giving away power in an appropriate fashion, an executive strengthens his or her *real* power by cementing relationships between leaders and followers.

Empowerment also needs to flow outward from the fire and emergency services to the community they serve. Fire and emergency services are beginning to recognize that they save more lives by preventing tragedies and reducing suffering then they ever will by responding. A community that receives education and training from its fire and emergency services professionals in subjects like CPR, first aid, and emergency preparedness and planning is less vulnerable and therefore less dependent on the responders. Cultural barriers are lowered because the community is claiming an organizational culture of inclusion for the greater good of all, a culture that includes those who serve and those who are being served.[24] Furthermore, empowering the community literally leads to the reduction of suffering and risk.[25] This goes to the heart of what it means to be a servant leader, to ensure that the least among us do not suffer.[26]

Let's summarize some of the key points about empowerment and servant leadership.

- Empowerment leads to individual satisfaction, a commitment to the organization, and retention, specifically in volunteer organizations.[27]
- Empowerment seems to enhance the experience of volunteers, and it is vital that the fire and emergency services hold on to those who are willing to serve just to serve.[28]
- Empowering individuals leads to higher job satisfaction, retention, motivation, and creativity.[29]
- By creating an atmosphere where the individual has a say in the future, empowerment instills pride and ownership within an organization and makes everyone a stakeholder.[30]
- Empowerment involves letting go of the reins and stepping aside so that followers can make decisions.[31] This is not about relinquishing all power and responsibility, but claiming a *different kind* of power gifted from followers whom the leader supports.[32]
- Empowerment is an act of trust.[33]
- There is a direct correlation between the involvement of followers in the decision-making process and superior performance.[34]
- Empowerment has a positive effect on followers' motivation and their creative processes.[35]
- Empowerment increases follower engagement in the operations of an organization and inspires them to reach high performance levels.[36]
- For the fire and emergency services, it is vital that responders remain physically and mentally strong to perform at high levels.[37]
- Burnout leads to lower performance levels that endanger not only the responder but also co-responders. The fire and emergency services leader can overcome this by empowering people and removing

the barriers that keep them from performing at their best.[38]

- Servant leadership means *not* doing business as usual, specifically by loosening centralized control.[39]
- One study found a direct relationship between the practice of servant leadership within an organization and future successes, with the essential component being abandoning—or at least adjusting—centralized control.[40]
- Instead of leading an institution with complete control, a leader who serves others can practice prudent faith, trust, and empowerment, then harness that gifted power and influence in order to foster others to lead.[41]

The final chapter will discuss how *service* is the center around which empowerment and all the other virtuous constructs revolve.

CHAPTER 11

SERVICE

"It's not about trying to find something to help you be a more effective leader. It's about trying to be a better person. The other will follow."

— James A. Autry

PATTERSON'S FINAL CONSTRUCT IS *SERVICE* AND IT BRINGS together everything discussed in this book, because all the other servant leadership characteristics and constructs are expressions of an individual's desire to serve. Deep down, a fire and emergency services responder desires to do good for others, recognizing this as the path for finding personal happiness and success.

Every major thoughtful leader who studies servant leadership learns that service is at the heart of what it means to be a servant-leader.[1] You can think of each of Spears' ten characteristics as part of a three-dimensional hologram where every characteristic—listening, empathy, healing, awareness, persuasion, conceptualization, foresight, stewardship, commitment to the growth of people, and building community—is a window to all the virtues of servant leadership.

Meanwhile, the first six virtuous constructs that Patterson identified—*agapao* love, humility, altruism, vision, trust, and empowerment—lead to the seventh and most essential construct: service. One does not simply reach service as if climbing to the top of a ladder and abandoning the rungs beneath it. The constructs do not flow in a linear direction. They form a continuous cycle of virtues, each of which is related to the other, and all of them based on serving others.

This final chapter will review the first six constructs and then summarize the argument for practicing servant leadership within the fire and emergency services.

The first of the seven constructs—*agapao* love—describes the moral love that inspires fire and emergency services responders to perform their often-dangerous—and sometimes deadly—duties.[2] In the course of one's career, a responder will experience horrendous situations, playing witness to humanity's tragedies. Love for one's fellow humans gives responders the strength to not only respond, but to *continue* to respond.

Agapao love is not a mushy emotion for fire and emergency services responders; it is a part of their *identity* that allows them to succeed and survive, because love conquers fear as they go forth into dangerous situations.[3] Love of their fellow responders and love expressed by their leaders is what allows them to feel safe.[4] The responder knows that even in the worst conditions, his or her fellow responders will give their all to save them from harm; this is love and it grants them comfort.[5]

Love matters because you cannot lead if you cannot love.[6] If you do not love your people, you cannot serve them. Followers need the love of a leader to overcome what stifles and trips them up.[7] Fire and emergency services responders need their leaders to serve them, to give to them everything they need to be successful, to willingly tear down the destructive bureaucratic model and replace it with a model of service, and this too is part of love.[8]

The second of the seven constructs is humility. Humility bonds people together through humanity.[9] Humility allows a person to see others not as "others" but rather as people. Humility leads to being an effective leader.[10] It overcomes narcissistic tendencies by viewing one's position with perspective. For the fire and emergency services leader, this means recognizing that you are in charge based upon your rank, yet you will be ineffective as a leader if your rank makes you believe that you are above your followers *as a person*. Because of your rank, you will receive a salute and a bigger paycheck; however, the rank does not make you a leader: your humility does.

The third construct of servant leadership is altruism. Out of altruism, leaders give themselves fully in service to their team. The needs of the followers become the needs of the leader, and the leader wants to meet their needs.

The decision to become a fire and emergency services responder is itself an altruistic choice. The profession is dangerous and the salary will not make responders wealthy. You could fairly say that a career within the profession is a sacrificial, benevolent act. The vast majority of those who currently serve—or seek to serve—within a fire and emergency services organization understand this from the beginning. Therefore, their decision to become a fire and emergency services responder rests on the notion that each of them desire to give of themselves in complete service of others.

The fourth construct Patterson identified was vision. The ability of a leader to vision is the key to the success of a leader.[11] For the fire and emergency services, vision begins with envisioning the emergency scene and possible outcomes. From that picture, a strategy emerges and tactics are decided. A leader's responsibility is to envision an outcome and make the decisions needed to accomplish that vision--foreseeing a solution to a problem.

Vision goes well beyond the emergency scene, however. It includes the ability to foresee the delivery needs of future services, which can only happen by having a picture of future needs of the community based on changing demographics and growth. A vision shared with the leader's team is the key to success of a fire and emergency services organization.[12] A shared vision instills pride of profession and a sense of personal ownership of the organization.[13] And by the way, setting and sharing the vision needs to be the responsibility of leaders *and* followers.

The fifth construct of servant leadership is trust. Successful relationships are built upon trust. A leader's trustworthiness stems from three attributes: ability, benevolence, and integrity.[14] A leader who lacks one of these three attributes loses trust. A leader who is not trusted is essentially powerless, and a powerless leader is a worthless leader.[15] Trust allows followers to grant power as a gift to a leader, and it must be reciprocated; leaders must also be able to trust their followers, and followers to trust each other.

Trust is the basis for teamwork, the foundation of successful fire and emergency services operations.[16] The fire and emergency services profession relies upon trust in tough situations. The last thing that an emergency scene needs is a group of responders who do not trust each other's abilities. In many ways, it is analogous to a battlefield situation;, the only way an emergency response can be successful is if each member of the team carries out his or her responsibilities and trusts the person next to them to do the same.

Patterson identified empowerment as the sixth construct of servant leadership. The practice of servant leadership embodies the idea of empowering others.[17] At its core, empowering is gifting followers the power to make decisions, a gift that comes in the form of trust. Empowerment is the decentralization of the decision-making process, allowing others to step up and lead.

In an earlier chapter, you learned how the fire and emergency services could not function without empowerment. Companies and crews often respond to incidents with small, mixed crews that may include junior officers, senior firefighters, or paramedics. Guiding them are policies and procedures created by the upper echelon of the organization, but each company or crew still needs to make decisions—Right now! On the scene! Executive level leaders need to empower and support followers; the very nature of the profession demands it.

The seventh construct of servant leadership—and a core message of this book—is service. Service drives the servant-leader, and the *desire to serve* drives fire and emergency services responders. Service means giving of self to others for something bigger than one's self.[18] The other six constructs identified by Patterson are building blocks for the individual to serve through concrete actions.

We now see the multiple parallels between servant leadership and the fire and emergency services. Fire and emergency services responders seek out the field from a desire to serve. Robert Greenleaf said that the natural impulse to serve, and serve first, is the motive of a servant-leader.[19] This work has identified how Spears' ten characteristics and Patterson's seven constructs mirror the attitudes and behaviors of the best fire and emergency services professionals. Servant-leaders in all professions do the same.

The fire and emergency services responder, and the organizations they represent, exist for a single reason: to respond to and serve the community to which they swore an oath. They conduct this service without question, judgment, or favoritism. The profession exists out of a love for one's fellow man and the product delivered to those served is benevolent and altruistic. The responder's humanity shows in their humility while carrying out their leader's shared vision. They function as a team in which they unreservedly trust each other *and* the leaders above them to respond in ways that provide the most effective service.

Values form the practice of servant leadership.[20] Values in the fire and emergency services reflect shared beliefs.[21] Values "form the foundation of the organizational culture and belief systems."[22] The highest values of the fire and emergency services are the same values that span successful organizations throughout the world, and the core value is service.[23] It behooves the fire and emergency services to adopt a leadership approach that models such universally-held beliefs, not because they are prescribed by a book on leadership, but because they *work*.

The purpose of this text was to introduce current and aspiring fire and emergency services responders to a leadership theory that resonates with the profession. This book establishes the groundwork for encouraging servant leadership by introducing virtuous constructs of the servant leadership philosophy and relating them to the values that form the career field. Perhaps those who read this will be inspired to take their desire to serve to the next step and become servant-leaders. It would have been easier to say that research found a direct correlation between the practice of servant leadership and job performance, or that the practice of servant leadership enhances organizational effectiveness.[24] Research, however, is not enough for arguing the need to become a certain type of leader. That must come from the head *and* the heart.

This book has presented ideas that are seldom taught in fire and emergency services training classes, such as persuasion, commitment to the growth of people, foresight, healing, and *agapao* love. These ideas used to be called "soft skills," as if they were nice, lovely ideas that had little to do with the nitty-gritty business of getting things done in the real world. But I am here to tell you that they are *hard* skills, and they have *everything* to do with operating effectively in the fire and emergency services. They require courage, humility, and maturity. The *real* "soft" skills are the easy outs—hiding behind regulations to avoid taking risks, ducking personal responsibility for one's team and the wider community, allowing a macho attitude to paper over genuine emotions, refusing to identify with the plight of others, and being dictatorial as a manager. Those behaviors are easy—and destructive to the individual and the organization.

Servant leadership is at the core of the fire and emergency services profession because the constructs live within individuals and give language to their desire to serve. If you are a current or aspiring fire and emergency services responder, you should have a shock of recognition as you read about humility, altruism, and trust because they are already part of your makeup, and you long to see them in your organization. They define what it takes to be a servant-leader.

This text is only the beginning of a leadership journey that will take a lifetime of hard work. The journey starts here by asking yourself: *What type of leader do I desire to be?*

References

Chapter 1

1. Sargent, C. (2006). *From buddy to boss: Effective fire service leadership*. Tulsa, OK: PennWell.

2. Seigal, T. (2006). Developing a succession plan for United States Air Forces in Europe fire and emergency services chief officers. *Executive Fire Officer Program*. Emmetsburg, MD: National Fire Academy.

3. Klinoff, R. (2012). *Introduction to fire protection*. Clifton Park, NY: Delmar.

4. Kirschman, E. (2004). *I love a firefighter: What every family needs to know*. New York, NY: Guilford Press.

5. Hiatt, E. (2010). *Analysis of servant-leadership characteristics: A case study of a for-profit career school president* (Doctoral Dissertation). Available from ProQuest Dissertation and Theses Database. (UMI No. 3389875)

6. Smeby, C. (2005). *Fire and emergency services administration: Management and leadership practices*. Sudbury, MA: Jones and Bartlett.

7. Klinoff, *Introduction to fire protection*.

8. Smeby, *Fire and emergency services administration*

9. Kirschman, *I love a firefighter*

10. Mills, C. (1959/2000). *The sociological imagination*. New York, NY: Oxford.

11. Kirschman, *I love a firefighter*

12. Mills, *The sociological imagination*.

13. Hiatt, *Analysis of servant-leadership characteristics*.

14. Smoke, C. (2010). *Company Officer*. Clifton Park, NY: Delmar.

15.   Walsh, D., Christen, H., Miller, G., Callsen, C., Cilluffo, F., & Maniscalco, P. (2005). *National incident management system: Principles and practices.* Sudbury, MA: Jones and Bartlett.

16.   McGee-Cooper, Trammell, and Lau, B., (1990). *You don't have to go home from work exhausted: The energy engineering approach.* Dallas, TX: Bowen & Rogers.

17.   Carter, H. (2007). Approaches to leadership: The application of theory to the development of a fire service-specific leadership style. *International Fire Service Journal of Leadership and Management,* 1(1), 27-37

18.   Patterson, K. (2003). *Servant leadership: A theoretical model* (Doctoral Dissertation). Available from ProQuest Dissertation and Theses Database. (UMI No. 3082719)

19.   Kirschman, *I love a firefighter.*

20.   Kirschman, *I love a firefighter.*

21.   Carter, Approaches to leadership, 27-37

Chapter Two

1.   Greenleaf, R. (1977/2002*). Servant-leadership: A journey into the nature of legitimate power and greatness.* Mahwah, NJ: Paulist Press.

2.   Russell, R., & Stone, A. (2002). A review of servant leadership attributes: Developing a practical model. *Leadership & Organization Development Journal, 23*(3/4), 145-157.

3.   Autry, J. (2001). *The Servant Leader: How to build a creative team, develop great morale and improve the bottom-line performance.* New York, NY: Crown Business.

4.   Spears, L. (2010). *Servant leadership and Robert K. Greenleaf's Legacy.* In Patterson, K., & van Dierendonck, D. (Ed.), *Servant leadership: Developments in theory and research* (pp. 11-24). New York, NY: Palgrave Macmillan.

5.   Greenleaf, R. (1970). *The servant as leader.* Indianapolis, IN: Greenleaf Center.

6.   Ibid.

7.   Hiatt, *Analysis of servant-leadership characteristics.*

8.   Bennis, W., & Townsend, T. (1997). *Reinventing leadership: Strategies to empower the organization.* New York, NY: Quill, William Morrow.
Kouzes, J., & Posner, B., (1993). *Credibility: How leaders gain and lose it, why people demand it.* San Francisco, CA: Jossey-Bass.
De Pree (2004). *Leadership is an art.* New York, NY: Doubleday.
Hunter, J. (2004). *The world's most powerful leadership principle: How to become a servant leader.* New York, NY: Crown.

9.   Blanchard, K. (1999). *The heart of a leader: Insights on the art of influence.* Tulsa, OK: Honor Press.
Hunter, *The world's most powerful leadership principle.*
Russell, V. (2009). Whitehall staff lack trust in managers' leadership. *Public Finance,* 6.

10.   McGee-Cooper, Trammell, and Lau, *You don't have to go home from work exhausted.*
Jaworski, J., (1996). *Synchronicity: The inner path of leadership.* San Francisco, CA: Berrett-Koehler.
Russell, and Stone, A review of servant leadership attributes, 145-157.

11.   Neuschel, R. (1998). *The servant leader: unleashing the power of your people.* East Lansing, MI: Vision Sports Management Group.

12.   De Pree, M., (1997). *Leading without power: Finding hope in serving community.* San Francisco, CA: Jossey-Bass.

13.   Bennis and Townsend, *Reinventing leadership.*
Greenleaf, *The servant as leader.*

14.   Autry, *The servant leader: How to build a creative team.*

15.   McGee-Cooper, Trammel, and Lau, *You don't have to go home from work exhausted.*

16.   Russell, R. (2001). The role of values in servant leadership. *Leadership & Organization Development Journal, 22*(2), 76-84.

17.   Covey, *First things first every day.*

18.   Ibid.

19.   McGee-Cooper, Trammel, and Lau, *You don't have to go home from work exhausted.*

20.   Greenleaf, *The servant as leader.*

21.   Bennis and Townsend, *Reinventing leadership.*
       Kouzes and Posner, *Credibility: How leaders gain and lose it.*

22.   De Pree, *Leading without power.*
       Hunter, *The world's most powerful leadership principle.*
       Kouzes and Posner, *Credibility: How leaders gain and lose it.*

23.   Hunter, *The world's most powerful leadership principle.*

24.   Blanchard, *The heart of a leader.*
       Russell, The role of values in servant leadership, 76-84.

Chapter 3

1.   Spears, L. (1996). Reflections on Robert K Greenleaf and servant leadership. *Leadership and Organizational Development Journal, 17*(7), 33-35.

2.   Ibid.

3.   Neuschel, *The servant leader: unleashing the power of your people.*

4.   Spears, Reflections on Robert K Greenleaf, 33-35.
      Spears, L. (2000). Character and servant leadership: Ten Characteristics of effective, caring leaders. *The Journal of Virtues & Leadership, 1*(1), 25-30.
      Spears, *Servant leadership and Robert K. Greenleaf's Legacy.*

5.   Covey, S. (1997). *First things first every day.* New York, NY: Fireside.

6.   Frick, D. (2011). *Greenleaf and servant-leader listening.* Westfield, IN: Greenleaf Center for Servant Leadership.

7.   Asbjörnson K, & Brenner M. (2010). Leadership is a per-
      forming art. *Leader to Leader. 2010*(55), 18-23

8.   Waterman, H. (2011). Principles of 'servant leadership'
      and how they can enhance practice. *Nursing Management -
      UK, 17*(9), 24-26.; DeGraaf, D.
      Tilley, C., & Neal, L. (2001.). *Servant-leadership charac-
      teristics in organizational life. Voices of servant-leadership
      series; booklet 6.* Indianapolis, IA: Greenleaf Center for
      Servant-Leadership.

9.   Blanchard, K., & Hodges, P. (2003). *The servant leader:
      Transforming your heart, head, hands, & habits.* Nashville,
      TN: Thompson Nelson.

10.   Ekundayo, J., Damhoeri, K., & Ekundayo, S. (2010).
      Presenting the servant leadership model as a panacea to bad
      leadership in tertiary education in West Africa. *Academic
      Leadership, 8*(4), 34.
      Undung, Y., & de Guzman, A. (2009). Understanding the
      elements of empathy as a component of care-driven leader-
      ship. *Journal of Leadership Studies, 3*(1), 19-28.

11.   Badea, L. & Panä, N. (2010). The role of empathy in de-
      veloping the leader's emotional intelligence. *Theoretical &
      Applied Economics, 17*(2), 69-78.

12.   Spitzer, R. (2000). *The spirit of leadership: Optimizing
      creativity and change in organizations.* Provo, UT: Executive
      Excellence Publishing.

13.   McGee-Cooper, Trammell, and Lau, *You don't have to go
      home from work exhausted.*
      Spitzer, *The spirit of leadership.*

14.   Autry, J. (1994). *Life and work: A manager's search for
      meaning.* New York, NY: William Murrow and Company.
      Ferch, S., (2004). *Servant-Leadership, forgiveness, and social
      justice.* In L. C. Spears, &; Pollard, C., (1996). *The soul of
      the firm.* Grand Rapids, MI: Zondervan Publishing House.
      Sipe, J., & Frick, D. (2009). *Seven pillars of servant leader-*

ship: Practicing the wisdom of leading by serving. Mahwah, NJ: Paulist Press.

15. Greenleaf, *Servant-leadership: A journey.*
    Spears, Reflections on Robert K Greenleaf, 33-35.
    Spears, Character and servant leadership: Ten Characteristics, 25-30.
    Spears, Servant *leadership and Robert K. Greenleaf's Legacy.*

16. Spears, L., & Lawrence, M. (2004). *Practicing servant-leadership: Succeeding through trust, bravery, and forgiveness.* San Francisco, CA: Jossey-Bass.

17. Fishkin, G. (1990). *Firefighter and paramedic burnout.* Los Angeles, CA: Legal Books Distributing.
    Sweeney, P. (2012). When serving becomes surviving: PTSD and suicide in the fire service. Retrieved from http://sweeneyalliance.org/grievingbehindthebadge/servingsurviving-sweeney/

18. Thurnall-Read, T., & Parker, A. (2008). Men, masculinities and firefighting: Occupational identity, shop-floor culture and organizational change. *Emotion, Space and Society,* 1, 127-134.

19. Braxton, E. T. (2009). Healing the wounded organization: The role of leadership in creating the path to social justice. *TAMARA: Journal of Critical Postmodern Organization Science, 8*(3/4), 89-118.

20. Greenleaf, *Servant-leadership: A journey.*

21. Covey, *First things first every day.*

22. Tate, T. (2003). Servant leadership for schools and youth programs. *Reclaiming Children & Youth, 12*(1), 33-39.

23. Lasky, R. (2006). *Pride and ownership: A firefighter's love for the job.* Tulsa, OK: PennWell.

24. Jensen, M. (2011). Nurturing self-knowledge: The impact of a leadership development program. *OD Practitioner, 43*(3), 30-35

25. Salka, J., & Neville, B. (2004). *First in, last out: Leadership lessons from the New York Fire Department*. New York, NY: Penguin.
     Thurnall-Read and Parker, Men, masculinities and fire-fighting, 127-134.

26. Hunter, *The world's most powerful leadership principle*.

27. Greenleaf, *Servant-leadership: A journey*.

28. Hunter, *The world's most powerful leadership principle*.
     Spears, Reflections on Robert K Greenleaf, 33-35.

29. De Pree, *Leading without power*.
     Hunter, *The world's most powerful leadership principle*.
     Liden, R., Wayne, S., Zhao, H., & Henderson, D. (2008). Servant leadership: Development of a multidimensional measure and multi-level assessment. *Leadership Quarterly, 19*(2), 161-177
     Sendjaya, S., & Sarros, J. (2002). Servant leadership: It's origin, development, and application in organizations. *Journal of Leadership & Organizational Studies, 9* (2), 57-64.;
     Spears, Character and servant leadership: Ten Characteristics, 25-30.
     Spears, L. (2004). *The understanding and practice of servant-leadership.* In Spears, L. & M. Lawrence (Eds.), *Practicing servant leadership: Succeeding through trust, bravery, and forgiveness.* San Francisco, CA: Jossey-Bass.
     Spears, *Servant leadership and Robert K. Greenleaf's Legacy*.

30. Hunter, *The world's most powerful leadership principle*.

31. Arfsten, D. (2006). *Servant leadership: A quantitative study of the perceptions of employees of a Christian-based, for-profit organization* (Doctoral Dissertation). Available from ProQuest Dissertation and Theses Database. (UMI No. 3226110). Sendjaya, S., & Sarros, J. (2002). Servant leadership: Its origin, development, and application in organizations. *Journal of Leadership & Organizational Studies, 9*(2), 57-64.

32. Atkinson, P. (2011). Change mastery. *Management Services, 55*(1), 23-28.

33. Greenleaf, *Servant-leadership: A journey.*

34. Spears, *The understanding and practice of servant-leadership.*

35. Bennis and Townsend, *Reinventing leadership.*
    Greenleaf, R. (1998). *The power of servant leadership.* San Francisco, CA: Berrett-Koehler Publishers, Inc.
    Spears, Reflections on Robert K Greenleaf, 33-35.
    Spears, Character and servant leadership: Ten Characteristics, 25-30.
    Stramba, L. (2003). Servant leaership practices. *Community College Enterprise, 9*(2), 103-113.

36. Greenleaf, *The power of servant leadership.*

37. Spears, Character and servant leadership: Ten Characteristics, 25-30.
    Spears, *The understanding and practice of servant-leadership.*
    Spears, *Servant leadership and Robert K. Greenleaf's Legacy.*

38. Sendjaya and Sarros, *Servant leadership: It's origin,* 57-64.

39. Bennis and Townsend, *Reinventing leadership.*

40. Greenleaf, *Servant-leadership: A journey.*

41. Blanchard, *The heart of a leader.*

42. Greenleaf, *Servant-leadership: A journey.*
    Stramba, Servant leadership practices, , 103-113.

43. Spears, *The understanding and practice of servant-leadership*
    Spears, *Servant leadership and Robert K. Greenleaf's Legacy.*

44. Barbuto, J., & Wheeler, D. (2006). Scale development and construct clarification of servant leadership. *Group Organization Management, 31*(3), 300-326.

45. Stramba, Servant leadership practices, 103-113.

46. Jennings, K., & Stahl-Wert, J. (2004). *The serving leader: Five powerful actions that will transform your team, your business, and your community.* San Francisco, CA: Bar-

rett-Kohler.
Stramba, Servant leadership practices, 103-113.

47.   Greenleaf, *The servant as leader*.
Greenleaf, *Servant-leadership: A journey*.
Spears, *The understanding and practice of servant-leadership*.
Spears, and Lawrence, *Practicing servant-leadership*.
Zohar, D., (2000). *Spiritual intelligence: The ultimate intelligence*. New York, NY: Bloomsbury.

48.   Hunter, *The world's most powerful leadership principle*.

49.   Blanchard and Hodges, The servant leader: Transforming your heart.

50.   Inbarasu, J. (2010). *Influence of servant-leadership practice on job satisfaction: A correlational study in a Lutheran organization* (Doctoral Dissertation). Available from ProQuest Dissertation and Theses Database. (UMI No. 3349273).
Spears, *The understanding and practice of servant-leadership*.
Spears, and Lawrence, *Practicing servant-leadership*.

51.   Ren, X. (2010). How to practice servant leadership. *Studies in Literature and Language, 1*(1), 7-10.

52.   Autry, *The Servant Leader: How to build a creative team*.

53.   Blanchard and Hodges, *The servant leader: Transforming your heart*.

54.   Liden, et al., Servant leadership, 161-177.
Keith, K. (2008). *The case for servant leadership*. Westfield, IN: Greenleaf Center for Servant Leadership.

55.   van Doren, J. A. (2006). Leading in a tactical paradise. *Fire Engineering, 159*(1), 12

Chapter 4

1.   Morris, J. (1955). *Fires and firefighters*. Boston, MA: Little, Brown, & Company.

2.   Fleming, R. (2010*). Effective fire and emergency services administration*. Tulsa, OK: PennWell.
Smeby, *Fire and emergency services administration*.

3.   Lasky, *Pride and ownership: A firefighter's love for the job.*

4.   Thurnall-Read and Parker, Men, masculinities and firefighting, 127-134.

5.   Thurnall-Read and Parker, Men, masculinities and firefighting, 127-134.

6.   Kirschman, *I love a firefighter.*
      Thurnall-Read and Parker, Men, masculinities and firefighting, 127-134.

7.   Floren, Impact of death and dying on emergency care personnel, 43-47.
      Rainone, P. (2000). Emergency workers at risk. Retrieved from http://www.emsvillage.com/articles/article.cfm?id=176

8.   Sweeney, *When serving becomes surviving,* http://sweeneyalliance.org/grievingbehindthebadge/servingsurviving-sweeney/

9.   Thurnall-Read and Parker, Men, masculinities and firefighting, 127-134.

10.   Sweeney, *When serving becomes surviving,* http://sweeneyalliance.org/grievingbehindthebadge/servingsurviving-sweeney/

11.   Anglin, G. (2001). *Company officer training and development-maintaining consistency in a dynamic environment.* Executive Fire Officer Program. Emmetsburg, MD: National Fire Academy.
      Coleman, J. (2008). *Incident management for the streetsmart fire officer.* Tulsa, OK: PennWell.

12.   Sargent, *From buddy to boss.*

13.   Salka & Neville, 2004
      Sargent, *From buddy to boss.*
      Seigal, Developing a succession plan for United States Air Forces.
      Smith, R. (1972). *Report from Engine Company 82.* New

York, NY: Warner Book.
Smoke, C. *Company Officer.*

14. Kirschman, *I love a firefighter.*

15. IAFC. (2011). *Chief officer: Principles and practice.* Burlington, MA: Jones and Bartlett Learning.;
Smeby, *Fire and emergency services administration.*

16. Fishkin, *Firefighter and paramedic burnout.*

17. Patterson, *Servant leadership: A theoretical model.*

18. Stone, A., Russell, R., & Patterson, K. (2004). Transformational versus servant leadership: A difference in leader focus. *Leadership & Organization Development Journal, 25*(4), 349 – 361

19. Smith, B., Montagno, R., & Kuzmenko, T. (2004). Transformational and servant leadership: content and contextual comparisons. *Journal of Leadership & Organizational Studies, 10*(4), 80-91

20. Stone, Russell, and Patterson, Transformational versus servant leadership, 349 – 361

21. Stanley, M. (1995). Servant leadership in the fire service: It's never lonely at the top when you're leading. *Fire Engineering, 148*(8), 30.

Chapter 5

1. Kerfoot, K. (2006). On leadership. Authentic leadership. *Nursing Economics, 24*(2), 116-117.
Farber, S. (2004). *The radical leap. A personal lesson in extreme leadership.* Chicago, IL: Dearborn Trade Publishing.

2. Bryant, J. (2010). Leading with love in a fear-based world. *Leader to Leader, 2*(56), 32-38.
Caldwell, C., & Dixon, R. (2010). Love, forgiveness, and trust: Critical values of the modern leader. *Journal of Business Ethics, 93*(1), 91-101.

3. Townsend, P. (1982). Love and leadership. *Marine Corps Gazette, 2*, 24.

4.   Farber, *The radical leap. A personal lesson in extreme leadership.*

5.   Fry, L. W., Vitucci, S., & Cedillo, M. (2005). Spiritual leadership and army transformation: Theory, measurement, and establishing a baseline. *The Leadership Quarterly, 16*(5), 835-862.

6.   Fishkin, *Firefighter and paramedic burnout.*
      Floren, T. (1984). Impact of death and dying on emergency care personnel. *Emergency Medical Services, 13*(2), 43-47.;
      Kirschman, *I love a firefighter.*
      Rainone, *Emergency workers at risk*, http://www.emsvillage.com/articles/article.cfm?id=176
      Sweeney, *When serving becomes surviving,* http://sweeneyalliance.org/grievingbehindthebadge/servingsurviving-sweeney/

7.   Fishkin, *Firefighter and paramedic burnout.*
      Sweeney, *When serving becomes surviving,* http://sweeneyalliance.org/grievingbehindthebadge/servingsurviving-sweeney/

8.   Sweeney, *When serving becomes surviving,* http://sweeneyalliance.org/grievingbehindthebadge/servingsurviving-sweeney/

9.   Love, C. (2005). Using both head and heart for effective leadership. *Journal of Family & Consumer Sciences, 97*(2), 17-19.

10.   Hoyle, J. (2002). *Leadership and the force of love: Six keys to motivating with love.* Thousand Oaks, CA: Corwin Press.

11.   Hoyle, J., & Slater, R. (2001). Love, happiness, and America's schools: The role of education in the 21st century. *Phi Delta Kappan, 82*(10), 790-794.

12.   McGee-Cooper, Trammell, and Lau, *You don't have to go home from work exhausted.*

13.   Covey, *First things first every day.*

14. Autry, J. (1991). *Love and profit*. New York, NY: Morrow.

15. Frick, D. (2004). *Robert K. Greenleaf: A life of servant leadership*. San Francisco, CA: Berrett-Koehler.

16. Winston, B. (2002). *Be a leader for God's sake*. Virginia Beach, VA: Regent University-School of Leadership Studies.

17. Bryant, Leading with love in a fear-based world, 32-38. Kerfoot, On leadership. Authentic leadership, 116-117.

18. Sargent, *From buddy to boss*
    Smoke, *Company Officer*.

19. Hoyle and Slater, Love, happiness, and America's schools, 790-794.

20. Russell and Stone, A review of servant leadership attributes, 145-157.
    Winston, *Be a leader for God's sake*.

21. Peters, T. (2008). Leadership is love: A passionate pursuit of excellence. *Leadership Excellence, 25*(3), 7.

22. Winston, *Be a leader for God's sake*.

23. Ibid.

24. McGee-Cooper, Trammell, and Lau, *You don't have to go home from work exhausted*.

25. Love, Using both head and heart for effective leadership, 17-19.

26. Gunn, B. (2002). Leading with compassion. *Strategic Finance, 83*(12), 10-12.; Hunter, *The world's most powerful leadership principle*.

27. Ferris, R. (1988). How organizational love can improve leadership. *Organizational Dynamics 16*(4), 41–51.

28. Williams, T. (2004). Lead by love. *Quality Magazine, 43*(1), 8.

29. Patterson, *Servant leadership: A theoretical*.

30. Baer, G. (2007). *Real love in the Workplace: Eight principles for consistently effective leadership in business.* Rome, GA: Blueridge Press.

31. Bryant, Leading with love in a fear-based world, 32-38.

32. Farber, *The radical leap. A personal lesson in extreme leadership.*

33. Baer, *Real love in the Workplace.*

34. Caldwell, Love, forgiveness, and trust, 91-101.

35. Lasky, *Pride and ownership: A firefighter's love for the job.*

36. Salka and Neville, *First in, last out.*

37. Morris, *Fires and firefighters.*

38. Dwinell, J. (2011, December 8). *Firefighter killed in Worcester three-alarm blaze.* The Boston Herald.

Chapter 6

1.   Hayes, M., & Comer, M. (2011). Lead with humility. *Leadership Excellence, 28*(9), 13;
Hunter, *The world's most powerful leadership principle.*

2.   Hayes, M., & Comer, M. (2010). *Start with humility: Lessons from America's quiet CEOs on how to build trust and inspire others.* Indianapolis, IA: Greenleaf Center for Servant-Leadership.

3.   Lee Hean, L., & Guat Tin, L. (2008). Humility as an educational paradigm in leadership development programs: The Singapore perspective. *New Horizons in Education, 56*(1), 14-19.

4.   Autry, *The servant leader: How to build a creative team.*

5.   Hayes and Comer, *Start with humility.*

6.   Owens, B. P., & Hekman, D. R. (2012). Modeling How to Grow: An Inductive Examination of Humble Leader Behaviors, Contingencies, and Outcomes. *Academy of Management Journal, 55*(4), 787-818.

7. Seigal, Developing a succession plan for United States Air Forces.

8. Thurnall-Read and Parker, Men, masculinities and firefighting, 127-134.

9. Hayes and Comer, *Start with humility.*

10. Lasky, *Pride and ownership: A firefighter's love for the job.*

11. Exline, J. (2012, March 22). *Humility and the ability to receive from others* The Free Library. (2012). Retrieved December 27, 2012 from http://www.thefreelibrary.com/Humility and the ability to receive from others.-a029381265

12. Spears, *Servant leadership and Robert K. Greenleaf's Legacy.*.

13. Exline, J. J., Campbell, W. K., Baumeister, R. F., Joiner, T., Krueger, J., & Kachorek, L. V. (2004). *Humility and modesty.* In C. Peterson & M. Seligman (Eds.), *Character strengths and virtues: A handbook and classification* (pp. 461-475). New York, NY: Oxford.

14. Greenleaf, *Servant-leadership: A journey.*

15. Krause, N. (2012). Religious involvement, humility, and change in self-rated health over time. *Journal of Psychology and Theology, 40*(3), 199.

16. Fishkin, *Firefighter and paramedic burnout.*
    Floren, Impact of death and dying on emergency care personnel, 43-47.
    Rainone, *Emergency workers at risk*, http://www.emsvillage. com/articles/article.cfm?id=176
    Salka and Neville, *First in, last out.*
    Sweeney, *When serving becomes surviving,* http://sweeneyalliance.org/grievingbehindthebadge/servingsurviving-sweeney/

17. Peters, A., Rowat, W., & Johnson, M. (2011). Associations between dispositional humility and social relationship quality. *Psychology, 2*(3), 155-161.

18. Ibid.

19.   Davis, D., Hook, J., Worthington, E., Van Tongeren, D., Gartner, A., Jennings, D., & Emmons, R. (2011). Relational humility: Conceptualizing and measuring humility as a personality judgment. *Journal of Personality Assessment, 93*(3), 225-234.

20.   Hilbig, B. E., & Zettler, I. (2009). Pillars of cooperation: Honesty-humility, social value orientations, and economic behavior. *Journal of Research in Personality*, 43, 516-519.

21.   Ibid.

22.   Ibid.

23.   Chan, C., McBey, K., & Scott-Ladd, B. (2011). Ethical leadership in modern employment relationships: lessons from St. Benedict. *Journal of Business Ethics, 100*(2), 221-228.

24.   Nielsen, R., Marrone, J., & Slay, H. (2010). A new look at humility: Exploring the humility concept and its role in socialized charismatic leadership. *Journal of Leadership & Organizational Studies, 17*(1), 33–43.

25.   Hare, S. (1996). The paradox of moral humility. *American Philosophical Quarterly, 33*(2), 235-241. ; Doty, J., & Gerdes, D. (2000). Humility as a leadership attribute. *Military Review*, 80(5), 89.

26.   Grahek, M., Thompson, A., & Toliver, A. (2010). The character to lead: A closer look at character in leadership. *Consulting Psychology Journal: Practice and Research, 62*(4), 270-290.

27.   Nielsen, Marrone and Slay, A new look at humility, 33–43.

28.   Undung and de Guzman, Understanding the elements of empathy, 19-28.

29.   Foster, J. (2009). Cultural humility and the importance of long-term relationships in international partnerships. JOGNN: Journal of Obstetric, *Gynecologic & Neonatal Nursing, 38*(1), 100-107.

30.   Hare, S. (1996). The paradox of moral humility, 235-241.

31.   Foster, Cultural humility and the importance of long-term relationships, 100-107.

32.   Klinoff, *Introduction to fire protection.*

33.   Dennis, R. & Bocarnea, M. (2005). Development of the servant leadership assessment instrument. *Leadership & Organization Development Journal, 26*(8), 600-615

34.   Hayes and Comer, *Start with humility.*

35.   Smeby, *Fire and emergency services administration.*

36.   Nielsen, Marrone and Slay, A new look at humility, 33–43.

37.   van Dierendonck and Nuijten, The servant leadership survey, 1-19.

Chapter 7

1.   Patterson, *Servant leadership: A theoretical model.*

2.   Monroe, K. (1998). *The heart of altruism: Perceptions of a common humanity.* Princeton, NJ: Princeton University Press.

3.   Hunter, *The world's most powerful leadership principle.*

4.   Monroe, *The heart of altruism.*

5.   Chander, P., Conley, J., & Vesterlund, L. (2010). Introduction to the special issue on leadership, altruism, and social organization. *Journal of Public Economic Theory, 12*(4), 603-608.

6.   Day, C. (2004). *The passion of successful leadership.* School Leadership and Management, 24(4), 425-437.

7.   Greenleaf, *The servant as leader.*
       Greenleaf, *Servant-leadership: A journey.*
       Greenleaf, *The power of servant leadership.*
       Moss, J. A., & Barbuto Jr., J. E. (2010). Testing the relationship between interpersonal political skills, altruism, leadership success and effectiveness: A multilevel model. *Journal of Behavioral & Applied Management, 11*(2), 155-174. Patterson, *Servant leadership: A theoretical model.*

Spears, Reflections on Robert K Greenleaf, 33-35.
Spears, Character and servant leadership: Ten Characteristics, 25-30.
Spears, *Servant leadership and Robert K. Greenleaf's Legacy.*

8.   Axelsson, S., & Axelsson, R. (2009). From territoriality to altruism in interprofessional collaboration and leadership. *Journal of Interprofessional Care, 23*(4), 320-330.

9.   Kirschman, *I love a firefighter.*

10.   Moss and Barbuto Jr., Testing the relationship, 155-174.

11.   Lengbeyer, L. (2005). Selflessness & cognition. *Ethical Theory & Moral Practice, 8*(4), 411-435.

12.   Ribar, D. C., & Wilhelm, M. O. (2002). Altruistic and joy-of-giving motivations in charitable behavior. *Journal of Political Economy, 110*(2), 425-457.

13.   Reed, L., Vidaver-Cohen, D., & Colwell, S. (2011). A new scale to measure executive servant leadership: Development, analysis, and implications for research. *Journal of Business Ethics, 101*(3), 415-434.

14.   Kerfoot, On leadership. Authentic leadership. *Nursing Economics,*116-117.

15.   Kouzes, and Posner, *Credibility: How leaders gain and lose it.*

16.   Matteson, J., & Irving, J. (2006). Servant versus self-sacrificial leadership: A behavioral comparison of two follower-oriented leadership theories. *International Journal of Leadership Studies, 2*(1), 36-51.

17.   Pekerti, A., & Sendjaya, S. (2010). Exploring servant leadership across cultures: comparative study in Australia and Indonesia. International *Journal of Human Resource Management, 21*(5), 754-780.
      Resick, C., Hanges, P., Dickson, M., & Mitchelson, J. (2006). A cross-cultural examination of the endorsement of ethical leadership. *Journal of Business Ethics, 63*(4), 345-359.

18. Pekerti and Sendjaya, Exploring servant leadership across cultures, 754-780.
    Resick et al., A cross-cultural examination, 345-359.

19. Chander, Conley, and Vesterlund, Introduction to the special issue on leadership, 603-608.

20. Dynes, R. (1994). *Disastrous assumptions about community disasters.* University of Delaware Disaster Research Center

21. Twemlow, S. (2001). Modifying violent communities by enhancing altruism: A vision of possibilities. *Journal of Applied Psychoanalytic Studies, 3*(4), 431-462.

22. Dynes, *Disastrous assumptions about community disasters.*

23. Batson, C. D. (2011). *Altruism in humans.* New York, NY: Oxford University Press.

24. Monroe, *The heart of altruism.*

25. Morris, *Fires and firefighters.*
    Salka and Neville, *First in, last out.*
    Smith, *Report from Engine Company 82.*

26. U.S. Fire Administration. (2013). *Summary incident report: Search and rescue fatalities February, 1990 to December 8, 2011.* Retrieved from http://apps.usfa.fema.gov/firefighter-fatalities/fatalityData/reportBuilder

27. U.S. Fire Administration. (2010). *Firefighter fatalities in the United States in 2009.* Retrieved from http://www.usfa.fema.gov/downloads/pdf/publications/ff_fat09.pdf

28. Ibid.

29. NIOSH. (2010). *Career lieutenant dies following floor collapse into basement fire and a career fire fighter dies attempting to rescue the career lieutenant.* Retrieved from http://www.cdc.gov/niosh/fire/reports/face200923.html

30. Smith, *Report from Engine Company 82.*

31. Day, The passion of successful leadership), 425-437.

32. Sargent, *From buddy to boss.*

Chapter 8

1.   Frick, *Robert K. Greenleaf: A life of servant leadership*.

2.   Whetstone, J. (2002). Personalism and moral leadership: the servant leader with a transforming vision. *Business Ethics: A European Review, 11*(4), 385-392.

3.   Frick, *Robert K. Greenleaf: A life of servant leadership*.

4.   Greenleaf, *Servant-leadership: A journey*.

5.   Spears, Reflections on Robert K Greenleaf, 33-35.
      Spears, Character and servant leadership: Ten Characteristics, 25-30.
      Spears, *Servant leadership and Robert K. Greenleaf's Legacy*.

6.   Wise, K. (2012). Vision and state health department public relations practitioners: Prepared to lead. *Public Relations Review, 38*(4), 592-599.

7.   Vinod, S., & Sudhakar, B. (2011). Servant leadership: A unique art of leadership! *Interdisciplinary Journal of Contemporary Research in Business, 2*(11), 456-467.

8.   Ibid.
      Fisher, J. (2004). Servant Leadership it's the vision to see, and ability to serve. *Executive Excellence*, 15-16.

9.   Greenleaf, *The servant as leader*.

10.   Vinod and Sudhakar, Servant leadership: A unique art of leadership, 456-467.

11.   Aryal, K., & Dobson, O. (n.d). A case study from the national disaster management institute in the republic of Korea. *The Australian Journal of Emergency Management, 26*(4), 34.

12.   Whetstone, Personalism and moral leadership, 385-392.

13.   McCuddy, M., & Cavin, M. (2009). The demographic context of servant leadership. *Journal of the Academy of Business & Economics, 9*(2), 129-139.
      Patterson, *Servant leadership: A theoretical model*.

14. Bogue, E. (2006). A breakpoint moment: Leadership visions and values for trustees of collegiate mission. *Innovative Higher Education, 30*(5), 309-326.
    Pelling, M. (2011). Urban governance and disaster risk reduction in the Caribbean: the experiences of Oxfam GB. *Environment & Urbanization, 23*(2), 383-400.

15. Morris, *Fires and firefighters.*

16. Fleming, *Effective fire and emergency services administration.* Smeby, *Fire and emergency services administration.*

17. Autry, *The Servant Leader: How to build a creative team.*

18. De Pree, *Leadership is an art.*

19. Early, J., & Davenport, J. (2010). Desired qualities of leaders within today's accounting firm. *CPA Journal, 80*(3), 59-62.

20. Bell, M., & Habel, S. (2009). Coaching for a vision for leadership: Oh the places we'll go and the things we can think. *International Journal of Reality Therapy, 29*(1), 18-23.
    Early and Davenport, Desired qualities of, 59-62.

21. Shekari, H., & Nikooparvar, M. (2012). Promoting leadership effectiveness in organizations: A case study on the involved factors of servant leadership. *International Journal of Business Administration, 3*(1), 54-65.

22. Hunter, *The world's most powerful leadership principle.*

23. Shekari and Nikooparvar, Promoting leadership, 54-65.

24. Smoke, *Company Officer.*

25. Coleman, *Incident management for the street-smart fire officer.*

26. Wis, R. (2002). The conductor as servant-leader. *Music Educators Journal, 89*(2), 17.

27. Fleming, *Effective fire and emergency services administration.*

28.   Hale, J., & Fields, D. (2007). Exploring servant leadership across cultures: A study of followers in Ghana and the USA. *Leadership, 3*(4), 397-417.

29.   Wise, Vision and state health department public relations practitioners, 592-599.
      Tate, Servant leadership for schools and youth programs, 33-39.

30.   Fishkin, *Firefighter and paramedic burnout.*
      Fleming, *Effective fire and emergency services administration.*
      Kirschman, *I love a firefighter.*
      Smeby, *Fire and emergency services administration.*
      Sweeney, *When serving becomes surviving,*
      http://sweeneyalliance.org/grievingbehindthebadge/serv-ingsurviving-sweeney/

31.   Park, S. (2012). If disaster struck, would you be ready to respond. *Hawaii Journal of Medicine & Public Health, 71*(9), 266.

32.   McCuddy and Cavin, The demographic context of servant leadership, 129-139.

33.   Tate, Servant leadership for schools and youth programs, 33-39.

34.   Vinod and Sudhakar, Servant leadership: A unique art of leadership, 456-467.

35.   Mehta and Pillay, Revisiting servant leadership, 24-41.

36.   Wis, The conductor as servant-leader, 17.

37.   Whetstone, Personalism and moral leadership, 385-392.

38.   Bell, and Habel, Coaching for a vision for leadership, 18-23.

39.   Fisher, Servant Leadership it's the vision to see, and ability to serve, 15-16.
      Park, If disaster struck, would you be ready to respond, 266.
      Whetstone, Personalism and moral leadership, 385-392.

40.   Anglin, *Company officer training and development.*
      Fleming, *Effective fire and emergency services administration.*

Chapter 9

1.   Caldwell, C. & Clapham, S. (2003). Organizational trust-
      worthiness: An international perspective. *Journal of Business
      Ethics, 47*(4), 349–364.

2.   Mills, *The sociological imagination.*

3.   Caldwell, Love, forgiveness, and trust, 91-101.

4.   Fletcher, M. (1999). The effects of internal communica-
      tion, leadership and team performance on successful ser-
      vice quality implementation: A South African perspective.
      Team Performance Management, 5(5), 150-163.

5.   Reina, D. & Reina, M. (2007). Rebuilding trust: The lead-
      er's role. *Leadership Excellence, 24*(2), 17–18.

6.   Ibid.

7.   Caldwell, C., Davis, B., & Devine, J. (2009). Trust, faith,
      and betrayal: Insights from management for the wise be-
      liever. *Journal of Business Ethics, 89*(1), 103–114.

8.   Hosmer, L. (1995). Trust: The connecting link between or-
      ganizational theory and behavior. *Academy of Management
      Review*, 20, 379–404.

9.   Ibid.

10.   Caldwell, C. & Hayes, L. (2007). Leadership, trustworthi-
      ness, and the mediating lens. *The Journal of Management
      Development, 26*(3), 261–274.

11.   De Pree, *Leading without power.*

12.   Cerit, Y. (2009). The effects of servant leadership behaviors
      of school principals on teachers' job satisfaction. *Educa-
      tional Management Administration & Leadership, 37*(5),
      600-623.

13.   Mills, *The sociological imagination.*

14.   Mills, *The sociological imagination.*

15.   Gayk, R. (2012). The "T" in team. *Fire-rescue Magazine, 30*(7), 70-71.;
       Mills, *The sociological imagination.*

16.   Caldwell, Love, forgiveness, and trust, 91-101.

17.   Ibid.

18.   Mills, *The sociological imagination.*

19.   Mills, *The sociological imagination.*

20.   Fletcher, The effects of internal communication, 150-163.

21.   Harbour, T. (2009). Trust through communications. *Fire Management Today, 69*(1), 4.

22.   Kramer, Trust and distrust in organizations, 569–596.

23.   De Pree, *Leading without power.*

24.   Kramer, R. (1999). Trust and distrust in organizations: Emerging perspectives, enduring questions. *Annual Review of Psychology, 50*(1), 569–596.

25.   Caldwell, Davis, and Devine, Trust, faith, and betrayal, 103–114.

26.   Klinoff, *Introduction to fire protection.*

27.   Alyn, K. (2008). The power of empowerment in leadership. *Firehouse, 33*(10), 88.

28.   Heidegger, M. (1962). *Being and time.* New York, NY: Harper & Row.

29.   Kramer, Trust and distrust in organizations, 569–596.

30.   Baran, B. (2010). Organizing ambiguity: A grounded theory of leadership and sensemaking within dangerous contexts. *Military Psychology*, 22, 42-69.

31.   Caldwell, Davis, and Devine, Trust, faith, and betrayal, 103–114.

32.   Caldwell and Hayes, Leadership, trustworthiness, and the mediating lens, 261–274.

33. Caldwell, C., Hayes, L., Karri, R., & Bernal, P. (2008). Ethical stewardship: The role of leadership behavior and perceived trustworthiness. *Journal of Business Ethics, 78*(1/2), 153–164.

34. Caldwell and Clapham, Organizational trustworthiness, 349–364.

35. Compton, D. (2010). Ethical behavior. The essence of trust and respect in navigating the political process. *Firehouse, 35*(5), 22.

36. Crosby, F. (2007). The real meaning of brotherhood. Fire Engineering, 160(7), 107. May, B. (2012). Marketing ICS. Building public trust by promoting what we do. *Firehouse, 37*(2), 94.

37. Sargent, *From buddy to boss.*

38. Caldwell et al., Ethical stewardship, 153–164.

39. Caldwell and Hayes, Leadership, trustworthiness, and the mediating lens, 261–274.
    Smoke, *Company Officer.*

40. Chung, J., Chan Su, J., Kyle, G., & Petrick, J. (2010). Servant leadership and procedural justice in the U.S. National Park Service: The antecedents of job satisfaction. *Journal of Park & Recreation Administration, 28*(3), 1-15.

41. Crosby, The real meaning of brotherhood, 107. May, Marketing ICS. Building public trust, 94.

42. Mills, *The sociological imagination.*

43. Fletcher, The effects of internal communication, 150-163.

44. Del, M., & Akbarpour, M. (2011). The Relationship between Servant Leadership of Managers and Employees Trust (Case Study: Guilan Province Public Organizations). *Interdisciplinary Journal of Contemporary Research In Business, 3*(6), 525-537. Joseph, E., & Winston, B. (2005). A correlation of servant leadership, leader trust, and organizational trust. *Leadership & Organization Development Journal, 26*(1), 6-22.

45.   Krajewski, B. (2004). Building a Culture of TRUST. *American School Board Journal, 191*(9), 32.

Chapter 10

1.   Russell, The role of values in servant leadership, 76-84.

2.   Dennis and Bocarnea, Development of the servant leadership assessment instrument, 600-615

3.   Asag-Gau, L., & Van Dierendonck, D. (2011). The impact of servant leadership on organizational commitment among the highly talented: the role of challenging work conditions and psychological empowerment. *European Journal of International Management, 5*(5), 463-483.

4.   Young-Ritchie, C., Laschinger, H., & Wong, C. (2009). The effects of emotionally intelligent leadership behavior on emergency staff nurses' workplace empowerment and organizational commitment. *Canadian Journal of Nursing Leadership, 22*(1), 70-85.

5.   Lasky, *Pride and ownership: A firefighter's love for the job.*

6.   Fishkin, *Firefighter and paramedic burnout.*
      Floren, Impact of death and dying on emergency care personnel, 43-47.
      Kirschman, *I love a firefighter.*
      Sweeney, *When serving becomes surviving,* http://sweeneyalliance.org/grievingbehindthebadge/servingsurviving-sweeney/

7.   Choo, S., Park, O., & Kang, H. (2011). The factors influencing empowerment of 119 emergency medical technicians [Korean]. Korean *Journal of Occupational Health Nursing, 20*(2), 153-162.

8.   Ndoye, A., Imig, S., & Parker, M. (2010). Empowerment, leadership, and teachers' intentions to stay in or leave the profession or their schools in North Carolina charter schools. *Journal of School Choice, 4*(2), 174-190.

9. Sweeney, *When serving becomes surviving,* http://sweeneyalliance.org/grievingbehindthebadge/servingsurviving-sweeney/

10. Buchen, I. (1998). Servant leadership: A model for future faculty and future institutions. *The Journal of Leadership Studies, 5*(1), 125-124.

11. Schneider, S. & George, W. (2011). Servant leadership versus transformational leadership in voluntary service organizations. *Leadership & Organization Development Journal, 32*(1), 60-77.

12. Cherif, A., Ofori-Amoah, B., Hanna, B. W., & Stefurak, L. (2010). Strengthening the academic department through empowerment of faculty and staff. *Academic Leadership, 8*(2), 1-9.

13. Alyn, The power of empowerment in leadership, 88.
    Smeby, *Fire and emergency services administration.*

14. Ibid.

15. Caldwell, Davis, and Devine, Trust, faith, and betrayal, 103–114.

16. Alyn, The power of empowerment in leadership, 88.
    Smeby, *Fire and emergency services administration.*

17. Caldwell et al., Ethical stewardship, 153–164.
    Caldwell, Davis, and Devine, Trust, faith, and betrayal, 103–114.

18. Kirschman, *I love a firefighter.*

19. Smoke, *Company Officer.*
    Fleming, *Effective fire and emergency services administration.*

20. Salka and Neville, *First in, last out.*
    Smeby, *Fire and emergency services administration.*

21. IAFC. *Chief officer: Principles and practice.*

22. Haraway III, W., & Kunselman, J. (2006). Ethical leadership and administrative discretion: The fire chief's hiring dilemma. *Public Personnel Management, 35*(1), 1-14.

23.   Ndoye, Imig, and Parker, Empowerment, leadership, and teachers', 174-190.

24.   Öner, Z. (2012). Servant leadership and paternalistic leadership styles in the Turkish business context: A comparative empirical study. *Leadership & Organization Development Journal, 33*(3), 300-316.

25.   Dhungel, R., & Ojha, R. (2012). Women's empowerment for disaster risk reduction and emergency response in Nepal. *Gender & Development, 20*(2), 309-321.

26.   Greenleaf, *The servant as leader.*
        Greenleaf, *Servant-leadership: A journey.*

27.   Schneider and George, Servant leadership versus transformational leadership, 60-77.

28.   Schneider and George, Servant leadership versus transformational leadership, 60-77.

29.   Cherif et al., Strengthening the academic department, 1-9.
        Ndoye, Imig, and Parker, Empowerment, leadership, and teachers', 174-190.
        Slack, F., Orife, J., & Anderson, F. (2010). Effects of commitment to corporate vision on employee satisfaction with their organization: An empirical study in the United States. *International Journal of Management, 27*(3), 421-436.
        Zhang, X., & Bartol, K. (2010). Linking empowering leadership and employee creativity: The influence of psychological empowerment, intrinsic motivation, and creative process engagement. *Academy of Management Journal, 53*(1), 107-128.

30.   Ndoye, Imig, and Parker, Empowerment, leadership, and teachers', 174-190.

31.   Patterson, *Servant leadership: A theoretical model.*

32.   Hunter, *The world's most powerful leadership principle.*

33.   Caldwell, Davis, and Devine, Trust, faith, and betrayal, 103–1144.

34.   Cherif et al., Strengthening the academic department, 1-9.

35. Zhang and Bartol, Linking empowering leadership, 107-128.

36. Zhang and Bartol, Linking empowering leadership, 107-128.
    Mehta, S., & Pillay, R. (2011). Revisiting servant leadership: An empirical study in Indian context. *Journal of Contemporary Management Research, 5*(2), 24-41.

37. Fishkin, *Firefighter and paramedic burnout.*

38. Alyn, The power of empowerment in leadership, 88.

39. Polleys, M. (2002). One University's response to the anti-leadership vaccine: Developing servant leaders. *Journal of Leadership Studies, 8*(3), 117-130.

40. Buchen, I. (1998). Servant leadership: A model for future faculty and future institutions. *The Journal of Leadership Studies, 5*(1), 125-124.

41. Polleys, One University's response to the anti-leadership vaccine, 117-130.

Chapter 11

1. Keith, *The case for servant leadership.*
   Spears, *Servant leadership and Robert K. Greenleaf's Legacy.*

2. Winston, *Be a leader for God's sake.*

3. Bryant, Leading with love in a fear-based world, 32-38.

4. Baer, *Real love in the Workplace.*

5. Ibid.

6. Hoyle, *Leadership and the force of love.*

7. Peters, Leadership is love: A passionate pursuit of excellence, 7.

8. Kirschman, *I love a firefighter.*

9. Hayes and Comer, *Start with humility.*

10. Autry, *The servant leader: How to build a creative team..*

11.   Greenleaf, *Servant-leadership: A journey.*
      Vinod and Sudhakar, Servant leadership: A unique art of
      leadership, 456-467.

12.   Early and Davenport, Desired qualities of, 59-62.

13.   Sargent, *From buddy to boss.*

14.   Caldwell et al., Ethical stewardship, 153–164.

15.   Caldwell, Davis, and Devine, Trust, faith, and betrayal,
      103–114.
      Reina and Reina, Rebuilding trust: The leader's role,
      17–18.

16.   Gayk, The "T" in team.

17.   Shekari and Nikooparvar, Promoting leadership, 54-65.

18.   Patterson, K. (2003). *Servant leadership: A theoretical model.*
      Sipe and Frick, *Seven pillars of servant leadership.*

19.   Greenleaf, *The power of servant leadership.*

20.   Stone, Russell, and Patterson, Transformational versus
      servant leadership, 349- 361.

21.   Bruegman, R. (2012). *Advanced fire administration.* Upper
      Saddle River, NJ: Pearson.

22.   Edwards, S. (2010). *Fire service personnel management.* Up-
      per Saddle River, NJ: Pearson.; Marinucci, 2009; Wallace,
      2006

23.   Wallace, M. (2006). *Fire department strategic planning:
      Creating future excellence.* Tulas, OK: PennWell.

24.   Bruegman, *Advanced fire administration.*
      Edwards, 2010; Marinucci, R. (2009). *Fire chiefs guide to
      administration and management.* Upper Saddle River, NJ:
      Pearson.
      Wallace, *Fire department strategic planning.*

25.   Indartono, S., Hawjeng, C., & Chun-His Vivian, C.
      (2010). The joint moderating impact of personal job fit
      and servant leadership on the relationship between the task
      characteristics of job design and performance. *Interdisci-*

plinary Journal of Contemporary Research In Business, 2(8), 42-61.

26.   Jones, D. (2012). Servant leadership's impact on profit, employee satisfaction, and empowerment within the framework of a participative culture in business. *Business Studies Journal*, 4(1), 35-49.

ABOUT THE AUTHOR

DR. ERIC JAMES RUSSELL IS A FACULTY MEMBER WITH UTAH VALley University's Department of Emergency Services, and a part-time instructor with the American Military University's Department of Public Service and Health. Eric retired early from the Department of the Air Force Fire and Emergency Services as a Captain, his service consisted of both active duty military and civil service as a Crash-Rescue-Firefighter. He holds a Doctorate of Education in Organizational Leadership and a Master of Science in Executive Fire Service Leadership from Grand Canyon University. Eric's research and writing involves servant leadership within the fire and emergency services. Eric serves as a consultant to Aircraft Rescue Fire Fighting (ARFF) organizations and also writes and speaks on aviation fire and emergency services operational and leadership issues.

You can contact Eric at **www.thedesiretoserve.com**

ROBERT K. GREENLEAF
CENTER FOR
SERVANT LEADERSHIP

www.greenleaf.org

Made in the USA
Las Vegas, NV
13 September 2021